God Has a
Wonderful
Plan for Your
Life

THE MYTH OF THE
MODERN MESSAGE

D0557309

Ray Comfort

Living Waters Publications
Bellflower, CA

God Has a Wonderful Plan for Your Life:
The Myth of the Modern Message

Living Waters Publications
P.O. Box 1172
Bellflower, CA 90706, USA
www.raycomfort.com
(800) 437-1893

No copyright, August 2000

ISBN 1-878859-25-0

Printed in the United States of America

Edited by Lynn Copeland

Cover, interior design, and production by Genesis Group
(design@genesis-group.net)

Cover illustration by Gustave Doré, *The Doré Bible Illustrations*,
Dover Publications, Inc.

Adapted from the book *Bride of Heaven, Pride of Hell*

To tell an unbeliever that God has a wonderful plan for his life can be seriously misleading…We need to adjust our presentation of the gospel. We cannot dismiss the fact that God hates sin and punishes sinners with eternal torment. How can we begin a gospel presentation by telling people on their way to hell that God has a wonderful plan for their lives?

—JOHN MACARTHUR

To Dan, Debbie, Michelle, Renee, & Nicole Moulton; Marc Campbell; Mark Cahill; and Mike Morton

My special thanks to Lynn Copeland for her invaluable editorial work.

Contents

Preface

As I waited to take off in a plane in the early 1980s, I noticed that someone had removed a newspaper from the seat pocket in front of me, leaving a small portion of the paper sitting precariously at the top of the seat pocket. I leaned forward, took hold of the two-inch-square piece of paper and mumbled in semi-jest, "Could be a word from the Lord." As I turned it over, my eyes widened as I read, "I have yet many things to say unto you, but ye cannot bear them now (John 16:12)." I remember being mystified by the words "ye cannot bear them now."

One year later I went into the deepest, darkest, most frightening experience of my life. It left me so broken, for over a year I couldn't even muster enough courage to eat a meal with my family. It took five long years to recover from the experience.

I now understand what the word "bear" means. In the original it means to "endure, declare, and receive." That terrible experience left me with a broken spirit. It brought me to a point where I could receive, endure, and declare the many things I had learned. This book is about those "many things."

CHAPTER 1

Phenomenal Growth

*W*e live in exciting times. All around us we are seeing signs of the end of the age. Nation is rising against nation. There are wars, earthquakes, famines, and violence. The Jews are back in Jerusalem. The city has become a "burdensome stone" to the nations. Jesus said that iniquity (lawlessness) would abound, and it certainly is. At the same time, we have seen the incredible phenomenon of the rise of megachurches with congregations in the tens of thousands. We have heard of *millions* coming to the Savior in Russia, China, and Africa. Pockets of revival have sprung up in the United States and different parts of the world. These *are* exciting times.

With all the excitement, it doesn't seem that many have noticed a few statistical inconsistencies. In 1996, a survey conducted by the Alan Guttmacher Institute in New York found that "eighteen percent of abortion patients describe themselves as born-again or evangelical Christians" (*U.S. News & World Report*, August 19, 1996). That is, of those who murdered their own child, nearly one in five professed faith in Jesus Christ. That is a little difficult to reconcile with the fact that Christians are supposed to love God and to love others as much as they love themselves.

In 1994, the Barna Research Group found further evidence that all is not well in the contemporary Church. A survey revealed that one in four American adults who said they were born-again believe Jesus "sinned" while He was on the earth. Think for a moment of the implications of such a theology. Here we have millions of "believers" who supposedly confess that Jesus is Lord, and yet they think He sinned. Therefore, they believe the Bible is inaccurate when it says that Jesus "knew no sin" (2 Corinthians 5:21), that He was "in all points tempted as we are, yet without sin" (Hebrews 4:15), and that He "committed no sin,

One in four American adults who said they were born-again think that Jesus "sinned" while He was on the earth.

nor was guile found in His mouth" (1 Peter 2:22). This also means that Jesus wasn't the "spotless" Lamb of God the Scriptures say He was. His sacrifice wasn't perfect, and when God accepted His death as an atonement for our sins, He sanctioned a "contaminated payment" and is therefore corrupt by nature.

Sadly, the only logical conclusion to which we may come is that these multitudes who profess faith in Jesus are, in truth, strangers to true regeneration.

Some years ago, the Barna Research Group revealed that sixty-two percent of Americans claim to have "a relationship with Jesus Christ that is meaningful to them." Yet a Gallup Poll taken around the same time found that, of those Americans who say they have a relationship with the Savior, approximately ten percent were what Gallup called "a breed apart":

> They are more tolerant of people of diverse backgrounds. They are involved in charitable activities. They are involved in practical Christianity. They are absolutely committed to prayer.

That sounds like *normal* biblical Christianity. That means

there is a great mass of people who say that Jesus Christ is meaningful to them, but who are not "a breed apart." They are not involved in good works, nor are they tolerant of others. Neither are they involved in practical Christianity nor committed to prayer. That means there are millions of people in America who insinuate that they belong to Jesus Christ, but whose lives don't match their claims. Another Gallup Poll found "very little difference in the behavior of the churched and unchurched on a wide range of items including lying, cheating, and stealing."

We are told that ninety-one percent lie regularly at work or home, eighty-six percent lie regularly to parents, and seventy-five percent lie regularly to friends (*The Day America Told the Truth*). A massive ninety-two percent own a Bible, but only eleven percent read it daily. Surveys also show that ninety percent of Americans pray, but eighty-seven percent do not believe in all of the Ten Commandments. To top it off, according to the Roper Organization, sixty-one percent believe that "premarital sex is not morally wrong."

When I find myself in a hotel, I usually channel-surf in an effort to find something wholesome. This often means crossing the polluted and shark-infested waters of MTV. If anything epitomizes this foul-mouthed, sexually perverted, depraved, blasphemous, and rebellious generation, it is MTV. An article in the December 1995 *Youth Leader* magazine stated:

> More Christian teens watch MTV each week (forty-two percent) than non-Christians (thirty-three percent), according to a Barna Research Group survey of evangelical teens.

The article went on to quote Barna surveys showing that of these same teens, sixty-five percent said they prayed daily. An amazing seventy-two percent believed the Bible. However, over a three-month period, sixty-six percent confessed that they had lied to a parent or teacher, fifty-five percent had had sex, fifty-five percent had cheated on an exam, and twenty percent either got drunk or had used illegal drugs.

A Christian youth leader was interviewed recently on a popular national radio program. He spoke with great concern of the fact that young people were "leaving the Church in droves." Then he cited the number-one reason they were turning their backs on God. He had taken a survey to find out why and discovered that it was a "lack of opportunity in the Church," inferring that the Church should get its act together and give young people more opportunity.

Ask any pastor if there is "opportunity" to serve within his church and he will no doubt tell you of the lack of people to teach Sunday school, to visit the sick and the elderly, to go out with the evangelism team, to clean the church building, etc.

The truth is, if someone is a "Judas" at heart, he will find *any* excuse to go back into the world. If Judas had been given a survey form to fill out, no doubt he would have had many justifications for his betrayal of the Savior and his falling away:

1. He was publicly humiliated by Jesus when he suggested giving funds to the poor.
2. He felt a deep sense of rejection because he wasn't part of the "inner circle."
3. He needed the money.
4. The Chief Priests made him do it.
5. The devil made him do it.
6. The responsibility of looking after the finances became too much for him.
7. He was abused as a child.
8. He had a betrayal syndrome.
9. He lacked a father figure.

10. He didn't think his actions would have the grisly repercussions they had.

There are some who don't believe that Judas was even a Christian. There is a good reason for this: Jesus said of him, "One of you is a devil." There's a good clue.

Judas Iscariot was a hypocrite—a *pretender*. He had no idea who Jesus was. He complained that an act of sacrificial worship was a waste of money. He thought the expensive ointment with which a woman anointed Jesus should have been sold and the money given to the poor. Jesus of Nazareth just wasn't worth such extravagance. In his estimation, He was only worth about thirty pieces of silver.

The Bible tells us that Judas was lying when he said that he cared for the poor. He was actually a thief, who so lacked a healthy fear of God that he was stealing money from the collection bag (John 12:6).

The Parabolic Key

When Jesus gave His disciples the Parable of the Sower, it seems that they lacked understanding of its meaning: "He said to them, 'Do you not understand this parable? How then will you understand all the parables?'" (Mark 4:13). In other words, the Parable of the Sower is the key to unlocking the mysteries of all the other parables. If any message comes from the parable, it is the fact that when the gospel is preached, there are true and false conversions. This parable speaks of the thorny ground, the stony ground, and the good soil hearer—true and false converts.

Once that premise has been established, then the light of perception begins to dawn on the rest of what Jesus said in parables about the kingdom of God. If one grasps the principle of the true and false being *alongside each other*, then the other parabolic teachings make sense: the Wheat and Tares (true and false), the Good Fish and Bad Fish (true and false), the Wise Virgins and the Foolish (true and false), and the Sheep and Goats (true and false).

After the Wheat and Tares parable, Jesus gave the Parable of the Dragnet:

> "Again, the kingdom of heaven is like a dragnet that was cast into the sea and gathered some of every kind, which, when it was full, they drew to shore; and they sat down and gathered the good into vessels, but threw the bad away. So it will be at the end of the age. The angels will come forth, separate the wicked from among the just, and cast them into the furnace of fire. There will be wailing and gnashing of teeth." Jesus said to them, "Have you understood all these things?" They said to Him, "Yes, Lord" (Matthew 13:47–51).

Notice the good fish and the bad fish were in the net together. The *world* is not caught in the dragnet of the kingdom of heaven; they remain in the world. The "fish" that are caught are those who respond to the gospel—the evangelistic "catch." They remain together until the Day of Judgment.

Judas was a false convert. It would seem that he was a thorny-ground hearer. The Bible says of the thorny-ground hearer: "The cares of this world, the deceitfulness of riches, and the desires for other things entering in choke the word, and it becomes unfruitful" (Mark 4:19). Some of these professing Christians stay within the Church; others leave it in "droves."

False converts *do* have a measure of spirituality. Judas did. He convinced some of the disciples that he did truly care for the poor. He *seemed* so trustworthy that he was the one who looked after the finances. When Jesus said, "One of you will betray me," the disciples didn't point the finger at the faithful treasurer, but instead suspected themselves, saying, "Is it I, Lord?" That's why it's not surprising that so few within the Body of Christ would ever suspect that we are surrounded by those who fall into the "Judas" category. However, alarm bells should go off when we look at statistics such as those just cited. A warning should sound when it seems that the Church ought to have massive political clout, but sadly lacks it when push comes to shove. With our millions of professed believers we can't even outlaw the killing of the unborn. Something is *radically* wrong. But before we look at the remedy, we are going to look at the cause.

CHAPTER 2

The Way Out of Problems

*I*n light of alarming statistics, few could deny that the Church as a whole has fallen short of the powerful, disciplined, sanctified Church we see in the Book of Acts. This has happened because the enemy has very subtly taken the focus off our message. Instead of preaching the good news that sinners can be made righteous in Christ and escape the wrath to come, the gospel has degenerated into the pretext that we can be made happy in Christ and escape the hassles of this life.

One of America's largest publishers recently produced a quality, full-color publication that epitomizes the promise of a hassle-free life. Entitled *Is There a Way Out?*, inside it reads:

> Everyone is looking for a way out of their problems. There's no easy way out. You won't get respect by joining a gang. You won't find love in the back seat of a car. You'll never find success by dropping out of school. And the chances are about one million to one that you'll win the lottery. If you're *really* serious about making your life better, then try God's way. God gets right to the source of most of our problems: sin.

It may sound admirable—and even biblical—to infer to sinners that Christianity promises "a way out of their problems," but it's just not true.

It seems that we are so entrenched in traditional evangelism that we don't equate *real* life with the message we preach. It's no exaggeration to say that the following words from the pulpit are commonplace in many churches each Sunday morning (I know from many years of itinerant ministry that this is often what happens):

God loves you and has a wonderful plan for your life. He wants you to have *true* happiness and to fill the God-shaped vacuum in your heart that you've been trying to fill with sex, drugs, alcohol, and money. Jesus said, "I have come that you might have life, and have it more abundantly." So come forward now and give your life to Jesus, so that you can experience this wonderful new life in Christ.

While they are coming, let's pray for the Smith family who lost their two children in a car accident this week. Brother Jones has been diagnosed with cancer. Remember to uphold the *whole* family. His wife had another miscarriage on Tuesday, and both of their other children are chronic asthmatics. Sister Bryant fell and broke her hip. She's such a dear saint—she's had trial after trial in her life, especially since the death of her husband, Ernie. Elder Chambers lost his job this week. That will make things difficult for the Chambers family, with his upcoming triple-bypass operation. Sister Lancing died of kidney failure on Monday night. Keep the Lancing family in prayer because it's their third tragedy this year.

How many of you this morning need prayer for sickness or have problems with depression? That many? You had better stay in your seats and we will have a corporate prayer.

Let me tell you about a few of my Christian friends who live in the real world. One went with his wife to a meeting. Their teenage son drove there alone. On the way home, my friend came across an accident, so he stopped to help. When he looked into the vehicle, he saw his beloved teenage son dead—impaled on the steering wheel.

The senior pastor of a church at which I was on staff was once asked to get out of bed at 3:00 a.m. to counsel a man who was waiting in his living room. As he stepped into the room, the man began to cut him up with a machete. The pastor almost died, and was irrevocably scarred both physically and mentally so that he is now unable to minister. He currently requires twenty-four-hour care.

Another pastor friend learned that his wife had multiple sclerosis. The crippling disease left him as the only one in the family able to take care of their three young boys. Then he was diagnosed with cancer.

One of my graphic artists married a woman whose Christian husband died of cancer, leaving her to raise five kids. The marriage was fine until she ran off with another man. She left my friend with the one child that was his. Sometime after that, someone broke into his home and beat him to a pulp. He had to be rushed to the hospital for treatment.

One other friend found his beloved wife dead, in utterly tragic circumstances I am not at liberty to print.

On June 19, 2000, five trainees with New Tribes Missions pitched a tent during a violent storm in Mississippi. Jenny Knapp, an attractive twenty-year-old, noticed that rain was causing the roof to cave in, so she lifted the tent pole to raise the height of the roof. Suddenly, a bolt of lightning struck the pole and tore through her body, giving her second-degree burns on her face, arm, and back. Her friends resuscitated her lifeless body and rushed her to the hospital where she was placed in the intensive care unit. The young missionary recovered, but is terribly scarred and partly blind. It is a sad fact of life, but in the real world, lightning falls on the just and the unjust.

At least one church I know of may have noticed the paradox. They were called "The Happy Church," but recently decided, for some reason, to change their name.

I think that if we still want to cling to "God loves you and has a wonderful plan for your life," we had better hide *Foxe's Book of Martyrs* from the eyes of sinners. Speaking of martyrdom, have you ever given thought to what it would be like to be huddling together as a family, as hungry and ferocious lions rush into a Roman arena? Have you ever considered what it would be like to be eaten by lions? I have. My fertile imagination runs wild. What do you give the lion to eat first—your arm? How long would you remain conscious as he gnawed on it?

Can you imagine the feelings you would have if you had led your loved ones in a sinner's prayer using the *wonderful plan* hook? Suppose you had read to them from a booklet by one well-known and respected man of God in which he said, "Everyone is seeking happiness. Why, then, are more people not experiencing this happiness? According to the Bible, true happiness can be found only through God's way." What would you tell your beloved family as you look into their terrified eyes? How could you reconcile the word "wonderful" with having the fierce teeth of a lion rip you apart, limb from limb?

These are terrible thoughts, but they are not merely my fantasies. Multitudes of martyrs have suffered unspeakable torture for the name of Jesus Christ. It shouldn't have been a surprise to the early Church when persecution hit them. Jesus warned them of the fact that they may have to give their lives for His name's sake. He even said, "Brother will deliver up brother to death, and a father his child; and children will rise up against parents and cause them to be put to death. And you will be hated by all men for My name's sake" (Matthew 10:21,22).

History tells us the fate of the apostles:

- Philip: Crucified, Phrygia, A.D. 54
- Barnabas: Burned to death, Cyprus, A.D. 64

- Peter: Crucified, Rome, A.D. 69
- Paul: Beheaded, Rome, A.D. 66
- Andrew: Crucified, Achaia, A.D. 70
- Matthew: Beheaded, Ethiopia, A.D. 60
- Luke: Hanged, Athens, A.D. 93
- Thomas: Speared to death, Calamina, A.D. 70
- Mark: Dragged to death, Alexandria, A.D. 64
- James (the Less): Clubbed to death, Jerusalem, A.D. 66

Persecution has always been the portion of the godly. According to Scripture, they have been "tortured,...had trial of mockings and scourgings, yes, and of chains and imprisonment. They were stoned, they were sawn in two, were tempted, were slain with the sword. They wandered about in sheepskins and goatskins, being destitute, afflicted, tormented —of whom the world was not worthy. They wandered in deserts and mountains, in dens and caves of the earth" (Hebrews 11:35–38).

Perhaps some may argue that the Christian life is a wonderful plan because God works all things out for the good of those who love Him (Romans 8:28). That fact is wonderful in the truest sense of the word. No matter what happens to a Christian, he can rejoice because of that promise.

In 1995, in Mainland China when Li De Xian was arrested for his faith, he no doubt knew that God would work all things together for his good. When he was beaten with a heavy club, kicked in the groin and stomach until he vomited blood, then beaten in the face with his Bible and left bleeding on the floor, the promise remained steadfast.

In 1413, John Huss was summoned to appear before the Roman church council in Constance. When he was thrown into a prison for nineteen months awaiting trial for his faith, he no doubt knew that God would work things out for his good. When he was burned alive at the stake and his charred, lifeless body fell among the ashes, the wonderful promise remained unwavering that God would work such an unspeakable horror out for his good.

According to a study by Regent University, in 1998 there were approximately 156,000 Christian martyrs throughout the world. The promise of God was also true for each and every one of these children of God.

When Moslems burst into churches in Rwanda in the late 1990s and hacked men, women, and children to death with razor-sharp machetes, if the many who bled to death loved God and were called according to His purpose, they too could claim this incredible promise.

See if you can find any of the disciples telling sinners that God loved them and had a wonderful plan for their lives.

If it is wonderful that our Creator does work all things out for good—that He brings good out of every agony suffered by our brethren—why then shouldn't we use that truth as bait when fishing for men? Simply because it's not biblical to do so. Go through the Book of Acts and see if you can find any of the disciples telling sinners that God loved them and had a wonderful plan for their lives. Instead, their hearers were guilty criminals—enemies of God who desperately needed righteousness, not to be told that they could enhance their lives with God's wonderful plan. To a sinner, "wonderful" has *positive* connotations, not *negative* ones of machetes, hatred, persecution, beatings, and martyrdom. If they respond to the message only to improve their lives, when persecution comes, they will be disillusioned and fall away from the faith. This is because many respond experimentally, simply to see if the wonderful life promised by Christians is as good as they make it out to be.

Jesus didn't shield the newly converted Saul of Tarsus

from what was in store for him as a Christian. He said, "I will show him *how many things he must suffer* for My name's sake" (Acts 9:16, italics added). Stephen was cruelly stoned to death for his faith. James was murdered with a sword. John the Baptist also felt the sharp steel of persecution. Down through the ages, Christians have been hated, persecuted, thrown to lions, and, like Huss, even burned at the stake for the sake of the gospel.

In light of Christians being burned to death for their faith in central Africa in February 2000, perhaps the message "God loves you and has a wonderful plan for your life" applies only to the United States. That may have been the case right up until the shooting death of Cassie Bernall on April 20, 1999. Cassie was shot in the head in Littleton, Colorado, when she said, "Yes" to the question, "Do you believe in God?"

If persecution and hardship are the realities of the Christian life, why in the world would *anyone* in his right mind choose to become a Christian? What would bring someone to the Savior if it were not the promise of a wonderful new life in Christ? We will look at this in the next chapter.

CHAPTER 3

A Lifestyle Without a Life

There is perhaps a rational answer to the question, "Does Jesus really solve sinners' problems?" If those who say that "Jesus solves problems" were "converted" under the same gospel they propagate, and did not repent themselves, then there may be some truth in what they are saying. If they continue to live in lawlessness, then they don't have a struggle with the world, the flesh, and the devil. They are friends of the world. They flow *with* it rather than *against* it, and therefore don't have "tribulation" in it. Because they don't "live godly in Christ Jesus," they don't "suffer persecution" (2 Timothy 3:12). They are not hated for His name's sake because their lives are no different from those who are in the world. They live in the flesh, and therefore don't struggle to deny the flesh.

Neither do they wrestle against the devil. In fact, he will be pleased with what he sees. They have "found religion," and think that by going to church an hour on Sunday morning they are now all right with God, assuaging their nagging consciences. They joined the fellowship of the church; they enjoy the music, the social activities, the friendship, and the many other benefits of modern Christianity, including what they think is assurance of everlasting life. They *have* found happiness in their new lifestyle—but they haven't found new life in Christ.

And here's the double tragedy from such error. When the Church declares the message that "Jesus gives happiness," it restricts its field of evangelistic endeavor to those in society who will be interested: *those who are not happy*—those with alcohol, drug, marriage, personality, and financial problems.

These "problem" people don't hear the message of sin, righteousness, and judgment, with the command to repent and flee from the wrath that is to come. Instead they hear that Jesus is the answer to their marriage, alcohol, drug, and financial problems. He is the One who can fill the God-shaped vacuum in their lives. They therefore fail to repent (because they haven't been told to), have a false conversion (Mark 4:16,17), and don't become new creatures in Christ. They do "name the name of Christ," but they don't "depart from iniquity" (2 Timothy 2:19). Rather, they bring their sins *and their problems* into the Church. This has the following sad effects:

1. Wearing out the pastor. Instead of being able to fully give himself to feeding the flock of God in the capacity of a shepherd, he finds himself forever counseling those who are "hearers of the Word only and not doers."

2. Tragically, the "happiness gospel" then has the laborers (who are already few in number) tied up in the function of being counselors and propping people up, when these problem people don't need counsel or prop-up. They need repentance.

After speaking of the many problems plaguing the modern Church, J. I. Packer says these insightful words:

> This is a complex phenomenon, to which many factors have contributed; but, if we go to the root of the matter, we shall find that these perplexities are all ultimately due to our having lost our grip on the biblical gospel. Without realizing it, we have during the past century bartered that gospel for a substitute product which,

though it looks similar enough in points of detail, is as a whole a decidedly different thing. Hence our troubles.

In a publication called *What Do You Want From Life?*, the conclusion is drawn that we all want to be happy. Despite the list of things cited—sex, money, friends, fame, love, and so on—the question is: Can we be *truly* and *continually* happy? The answer is, of course, that knowing Jesus produces "ultra happiness...your happiest moment magnified a million times over."

Not many would see that there is anything wrong with this publication. However, the call of the gospel is universal, and not confined to the unhappy, "hurting" world, as it is so often promoted. The gospel is a promise of *righteousness*, not a promise of happiness, and it therefore may also be offered to those who are *enjoying* the "pleasures of sin for a season." Before my conversion, I was very happy, content, satisfied, cheerful, thankful, and joyful. I was loving life, and living it to the fullest. *Therefore, I was not a candidate for the modern gospel.* However, when I was confronted by the spirituality of God's Law and understood that

The call of the gospel is universal, and not confined to the unhappy, "hurting" world, as it is so often promoted.

"riches do not profit in the day of wrath, but *righteousness* delivers from death" (Proverbs 11:4), I saw my need of the Savior.

Let me repeat: Because of the belief that the chief end of the gospel is man's happiness on earth, rather than his righteousness, many fail to see its God-given intention. They think the gospel is only for those who lack money, those who are brokenhearted by life's difficulties, those who are the problem people in society. The belief is further pervaded through popular worship choruses that have splendid melodies, but carry this message: "Heartaches, broken people, ruined lives is why You died on Calvary." Again, like many others, before I became a Christian my life was not "ruined." At the age of twenty I was a successful businessman, with my own house, beautiful wife, car, money, and the freedom (being self-employed) to enjoy it to the full.

Evangelistic outreaches are billed as taking the Good News to "the hurting and the needy." Let me repeat: The gospel is not confined to the "hurting" people with ruined lives and heartaches. Both hurting *and* happy people need to be shown their sinful state before God, so they will seek after the righteousness that is in Christ.

Let me further illustrate this common misunderstanding by quoting from another modern publication (I am in no way questioning the sincerity of the author):

> You will desire to be where the Lord is. And He spends His time with those who hurt. At the beginning of His ministry, Jesus quoted Isaiah to describe the work He was called to do: "The Spirit of the Lord is upon me, because He has anointed me to preach the gospel to the poor; He has sent me to heal the brokenhearted, to preach deliverance to the captives, and recovery of sight to the blind, to set at liberty them that are oppressed, to preach the acceptable year of the Lord" (Luke 4:18,19) …Thus the more you go after God, the deeper you will move into a world filled with hurting people.

In Luke 4:18,19, Jesus gives us a summation of who the gospel is for:

- The poor
- The brokenhearted
- The captives
- The blind
- The oppressed

A quick study will show that Jesus is not necessarily speaking of those who lack financial resources when He speaks of the *poor*. The word means "meek, humble, lowly" —the "poor in spirit" (Matthew 5:3). These are the blessed ones to whom the kingdom of God belongs. The poor are those who know that they are destitute of righteousness. Bible commentator Matthew Henry said of this verse: "To whom He was to preach: to the poor; to those that were *poor in the world*; to those that were *poor in spirit*, to the meek and humble, and to those that were truly sorrowful for sin" (*Matthew Henry's Commentary*, Zondervan Publishing House, p. 1425).

When He speaks of the *brokenhearted*, He doesn't mean those unhappy people whose hearts are aching because they have been jilted by a sweetheart, but those who, like Peter and Isaiah, are contrite and sorrowing for their sin.

Listen to the respected Bible commentator once again: "For He was sent to heal the brokenhearted, to give peace to those that were troubled and humbled for sins, and to bring them to rest who were weary and heavy-laden, under the burden of guilt and corruption."

The *captives* are those "taken captive by [the devil] to do his will" (2 Timothy 2:26).

The *blind* are those whom "the god of this age has blinded ... [to] the light of the gospel of the glory of Christ" (2 Corinthians 4:4).

The *oppressed* are those who are "oppressed by the devil" (Acts 10:38).

The gospel of grace is for the humble, not the proud. God resists the proud, but gives grace to the humble (James 4:6). The Scriptures tell us, "Everyone who is proud in heart is an abomination to the Lord" (Proverbs 16:5). He has put down the mighty from their thrones, and exalted the lowly (Luke 1:52). God looks on the man who is poor and of a contrite spirit, and who trembles at His word (Isaiah 66:2). Only the sick need a physician, and only those who are convinced of the disease of sin will appreciate and appropriate the cure of the gospel.

The Abundant Life

Still, the question may arise, why not use the fact that Jesus said He had come to bring us an abundant life (John 10:10) to draw sinners to the Savior? True, the Christian life is full. Consider the life of Paul. Read 2 Corinthians 11:23–28 and see if you think he was bored while being stoned (once), shipwrecked (three times), beaten (three times), and whipped (five times). His life *was* full. There were also times he wasn't happy. In fact, at one point he was in such despair that he wanted to die (2 Corinthians 1:8).

The apostle gives the carnal-minded Corinthians a glimpse of the abundant life. He told them that he had been condemned to death. He was hungry and thirsty. He lacked clothing. He was beaten and had nowhere to live. Even with his established ministry, he was forced to work with his hands. He was reviled, persecuted, slandered, and treated as the filth of the world. What a terrible, uninviting path Paul walked down. One would think that he would put up a sign saying, "Don't enter here." However, he did the opposite. He told the Corinthians to imitate him (1 Corinthians 4:9–16).

Where is God's Love?

How was it, then, that the apostle Paul knew God loved him? As we have seen, he was whipped, beaten, stoned, and so depressed that at one point he wanted to die. He was mocked, hated, shipwrecked, imprisoned for years, and then finally martyred. What did he look to for assurance of God's love for him?

He didn't look at his lifestyle because, to the unlearned eye, it didn't exactly speak of God's caring hand for him. His "abundant" life was certainly full, but it wasn't full of what we think it should have been, if God loved him. Picture Paul, lying half-naked on a cold dungeon floor, chained to hardened Roman guards. Look at his bloody back and his bruised, swollen face. "Paul, you've been beaten again. Where are your friends? Demas and the others have forsaken you. Where is your expensive chariot and your successful building program? Where is the evidence of God's blessing, Paul?" you taunt. "What's that? What did you say? Did I hear you mumble through swollen lips that God loves you?"

Paul slowly lifts his head. His blackened, bruised eyes look deeply into yours. They sparkle as he says two words: "...the cross!" He painfully reaches into his blood-drenched tunic and carefully pulls out a large letter he had been writing in his own hand. His trembling and bloodstained finger points to one sentence in particular. You strain your eyes in the dim light and read, "I have been crucified with Christ; it is no longer I who live, but Christ lives in me; and the life which I now live in the flesh I live by faith in the Son of God, *who loved me and gave Himself for me*" (Galatians 2:20, italics added).

That was the source of Paul's joy, and thus his strength: "God forbid that I should glory except in the cross" (Galatians 6:14). Those who come through the door of seeking happiness in Christ will think that their happiness is evidence of God's love. They may even think that God has forsaken them when trials come and their happiness leaves. But those who look to the cross as a token of God's love will never doubt His steadfast devotion to them.

If the "abundant" life means something different from a "happy" life, who is going to listen if we are blatantly honest about the trials of living "godly in Christ Jesus" (2 Timothy 3:12)? Certainly not as many as are attracted by the talk of a wonderful plan. What, then, is the answer to this dilemma?

CHAPTER 4

The Purpose of the Law

*W*ho on earth is going to embrace our message if we don't use the promise of an abundant, wonderful new life in Christ? The answer to our dilemma is simply to do what Jesus did. It seems that the whole of the contemporary Church is running around with T-shirts, placards, stickers, books, wristbands, etc., asking the question "What Would Jesus Do?" They ask this for everything *but* evangelism. What did Jesus do when He confronted a sinner? He made the issue one of *righteousness* rather than happiness. He used the Ten Commandments to show sinners the righteous standard of God.

In Mark 10:17, a man came running to Jesus, knelt before Him, and asked how he could obtain everlasting life. This man came "running." He "knelt" before the Savior. It would seem that his earnest and humble heart made him a prime candidate as a potential convert. Yet Jesus didn't give him the message of God's grace. He didn't even mention the love of God. Neither did He tell him of an abundant, wonderful new life. Instead, He used the Law of God to expose his hidden sin. This man was a transgressor of the First of the Ten Commandments. His money was his god, and you cannot serve both God and money. Then the Scriptures reveal that it was *love* that motivated Jesus to speak in this way to this rich young man (Mark 10:21).

Every time we witness to someone, we should challenge our motives. Do we love the sinner enough to make sure his conversion is genuine; or do we love the feeling of getting another decision for Jesus, when in truth our zeal without knowledge has just produced another potential Judas?

Why did Jesus take the time to use the Ten Commandments? His method seems a little archaic compared to the quick and easy instant converts of modern methods. Dr. Martyn Lloyd-Jones gives us the answer:

> A gospel which merely says "Come to Jesus," and offers Him as a Friend, and offers a marvelous new life, without convincing of sin, is not New Testament evangelism. (The essence of evangelism is to start by preaching the Law; and it is because the Law has not been preached that we have had so much superficial evangelism.) True evangelism...must always start by preaching the Law.

When you use the Law (the Ten Commandments) to show the world their true state, get ready for them to thank you. For the first time in their lives, they will see the Christian message as an expression of love and concern for their eternal welfare rather than of merely proselytizing for a better lifestyle while on this earth. They begin to understand why they should be *concerned* about their eternal salvation. The Law shows them that they are condemned by God. It even makes them a little fearful.

Look at how John Wesley reconciles the use of the Law (to produce the fear of God) with love:

> The second use [of the Law] is to bring him unto life, unto Christ that he may live. It is true, in performing both these offices, it acts the part of a severe schoolmaster. *It drives us by force, rather than draws us by love. And yet love is the spring of all.* It is the spirit of love which, by this painful means, tears away our confidence in the flesh, which leaves us no broken reed whereon to trust,

and so constrains the sinner, stripped of all to cry out in the bitterness of his soul or groan in the depth of his heart, "I give up every plea beside, Lord, I am damned; but thou hast died" (italics added).

Perhaps you are tempted to say that we should *never* condemn sinners. However, Scripture tells us that they are *already* condemned (John 3:18). All the Law does is show them their true state. If you dust a table in your living room and think it is dust-free, try pulling back the curtains and letting in the early morning sunlight. You will more than likely see dust still sitting on the table. The sunlight didn't create the dust, *it merely exposed it.* When we take the time to draw back the high and heavy curtains of the Holy of Holies and let the light of God's Law shine upon the sinner's heart, all that happens is that the Law shows him his true state before God. Proverbs 6:23 tells us that "the Commandment is a lamp and the Law is light."

It was the wrath of the Law that showed the adulterous woman that she was condemned. She found herself between a rock and a hard place. Without those heavy rocks waiting to pound her sinful flesh, she may have died in her sins and gone to hell. I doubt if she would have fallen at the feet of Jesus without the terror of the Law having driven her there. Thank God that it awakened her and caused her to flee to the Savior.

The sinner thinks that he is rich in virtue, but the Law shows him that he is morally bankrupt. If he doesn't declare bankruptcy, the Law will mercilessly call for his last drop of blood.

What About Legalism?

One evening when I had taken a team to Santa Monica to preach the gospel, it began raining. It not only rained, but the heavens flashed with lightning. Thunder seemed to shake the earth in an unusually severe thunderstorm for Southern California. As a consolation for our team, we purchased two large pizzas to snack on as we took shelter from the pelting rain under a movie theater veranda.

As most of the thirty-member team munched on pepperoni pizza, I noticed the heartwarming sight of an elderly homeless woman having a fight with a ten-inch piece of cheese. It looked like a stretched rubber band as she pulled at it with what teeth she had left. I smiled at her and asked if she wanted me to get her a pair of scissors. Amid the battle, she was able to return a courteous smile.

After she had downed the large slice of pizza, I offered her another one. Surprisingly, she declined. A few minutes later, however, she was battling a second piece. The scene *was* truly heartwarming.

Suddenly, the police arrived. The theater manager had called the law and told them he wanted the woman removed. There were thirty of us sheltering from the rain, yet he had sorted out a poor, hungry, homeless woman, and was telling the police to force her to move away! I heard the officers protesting that she was just sheltering from the rain. The manager was adamant: the woman had to move on.

At that moment I remembered that my pocket was bulging with a bundle of one-dollar bills. Each Friday night I would pull in a crowd by asking trivia questions and giving dollar bills to those who answered correctly. Once the crowd felt comfortable, I would swing from the natural to the spiritual and preach the gospel. As the police officers (reluctantly) began to move the old woman on, I stepped forward and grabbed her hand. She flinched and swung her fear-filled eyes toward mine, probably thinking that she was being handcuffed. Then she noticed that I had stuffed a wad of bills in her hand, and in a second her fear changed to joy.

The Bible tells us in 1 Timothy 1:8, "Now we recognize

and know that the Law is good if anyone uses it lawfully [for the purpose for which it was designed]" (Amplified). Just as the theater manager had used the law for something for which it was never designed—turning an elderly homeless woman out into the rain—so there are those who would use God's Law for something for which it was never designed.

For what purpose was God's Law designed? The following verse tells us: "The Law is not made for a righteous person, but...for sinners" (1 Timothy 1:9,10). It even lists the sinners for us: the disobedient, the ungodly, murderers, fornicators, homosexuals, kidnappers, liars, etc. The Law's main design is not for the saved, but for the unsaved. It was given as a "schoolmaster" to bring us to Christ. It was designed primarily as an evangelistic tool.

The Law's rightful purpose is simply to act as a mirror to show us that we need cleansing.

It is an *unlawful* use of the Law to seek to use it for "justification." The Scriptures make that very clear: "A man is not justified by the works of the law but by faith in Jesus Christ...; for by the works of the law no flesh shall be justified" (Galatians 2:16). The Law's rightful purpose is simply to act as a mirror to show us that we need cleansing. Those who seek to be justified by the Law are taking the mirror off the wall and trying to wash themselves with it.

Neither should the Law be used to produce something we call "legalism." We are given incredible liberty in Christ (Galatians 5:1), and there are those who would seek to steal that liberty by placing the Law on the back of Christians. Obviously a Christian refrains from "lawlessness." He doesn't lie, steal, kill, commit adultery, etc. However, his motivation for holy living isn't one of legalism imposed on him by the Law. Why does he refrain from sin—to gain God's favor? No.

He already has that in Christ. He lives a life that is pleasing to God *because he wants to do all he can to show God gratitude for the incredible mercy he has received through the gospel.* His motive is love, not legalism. D. L. Moody said, "The Law can only chase a man to Calvary, no further."

Why then would any Christian stray into legalism? Why would he begin telling believers what they can and cannot do in Christ? This happens simply because the Law hasn't been used lawfully in the first place. Let me try to explain what I mean. If the spiritual nature of the Law is used in evangelism, it will once and for all rid a new believer of any thought of legalism. The Law reveals to him that there is no way he can please God outside of faith in Jesus. As he stands before the ground-shaking thunder and vivid lightning of Mount Sinai, it dawns on him that a holy Creator sees his wicked thoughts. He cringes as he begins to understand that God sees lust as adultery and hatred as murder. The guilty sinner sees that he is "by nature a child of wrath," and therefore flees to shelter in Christ from the rain of God's indignation. He knows that grace, and grace alone, saves him. Nothing in his hand he brings, simply to the cross he clings.

The true believer is saved knowing that *nothing* commends him to God. After a lifetime of good works, of reading the Word, of prayer and seeking the lost, he is still saved by grace and grace alone. He is an "unprofitable servant" who merely does what he should.

However, he who makes a commitment to Christ without the Law usually comes because he is seeking true inner peace and lasting fulfillment. He comes to fill a God-shaped vacuum in his life. There is no trembling. There is no fleeing from wrath. There is no fear. To him, God is a benevolent, fatherly figure, not wrath-filled. The Law hasn't stripped him of self-righteousness. He doesn't truly believe that his just reward is eternal damnation. Therefore, even as a professing

Christian, he thinks that he is basically a good person.

Because of this, he is the one who is likely to think that he is pleasing God by reading his Bible, praying, fasting, and doing good works. He is the one deceived into thinking that somehow his good works commend him to God, and he is therefore the one who is liable to stray into "touch not, taste not, handle not" (Colossians 2:16–23).

The Law, when used lawfully, liberates the believer from legalism. If, however, it is neglected before the cross, those who profess faith in Christ are prone to go astray into legalism and then impose demands on other believers, stealing from them the great liberty we have in Christ.

Look at the function of the Law from the great classic *Pilgrim's Progress* by John Bunyan:

> "It was he [the Law] who did bind my heavy burden upon me." Faithful agrees: "Aye. Had it not been for him, we had both of us stayed in the City of Destruction."
>
> "Then he did us a favor," answered Christian. [Faithful then shows how the Law alarms us:] "Aye. Albeit, he did it none too gently." Then Christian says, "Well, at least he played the part of a schoolmaster and showed us our need. It was he who drove us to the cross."

There are many wonderful references to the work of the Ten Commandments hidden within the pages of God's Word. We will unveil some of these in the next chapter.

CHAPTER 5

Our Broken Backbone

There are two reasons why the Church would seem to be full of people whose lives don't live up to what they should. As we have seen, the modern gospel has degenerated into a means of happiness, rather than one of righteousness. Second, we have failed to show the sinner that he is a lawbreaker, that he has violated the Law of a holy God.

When I speak of using the Law in evangelism, I am not speaking of a mere casual reference to it, but as the backbone of the gospel presentation, because its function is to prepare the heart for grace. Martin Luther said of the Law, "In its true and proper work and purpose it humbles a man and prepares him—if he uses the Law correctly—to yearn and seek for grace." The Law is the rod and staff of the shepherd to guide the sheep to himself. It is the net of the fisherman, and the hoe of the farmer. It is the ten golden trumpets that prepare the way for the king. The Law makes the sinner thirst for righteousness, that he might live. Its holy light reveals the dust of sin on the table of the human heart, so that the gospel in the hand of the Spirit can wipe it perfectly clean.

The Law should be esteemed by the Church because of its wonderful preparatory work in preparing a sinner's heart for grace. In Joshua 3:14–17, God opened the Jordan River when the feet of the priests, who were carrying the ark of the covenant, touched its waters. Do you remember what the ark contained? It was the two tablets of God's Law. Do you think that God would have opened the waters for the priests if they had complained that the two stone tablets were too heavy, and tipped them into the dirt to make their load lighter? Yet that is what many in the contemporary Church have done. The Law is the embodiment of this gospel we carry, but many have "neglected the weightier matters of the Law" and counted them as worthless. They have emptied the ark of the gospel, stripping it of its power.

J. C. Ryle said of God's Law, "But never, never let us despise it. It is the symptom of an ignorant ministry, and unhealthy state of religion, when the Law is reckoned unimportant. The true Christian delights in God's Law (Romans 7:22)."

The Ten Commandments are like the ten camels that carried Abraham's servant in search of a bride for his only begotten son, Isaac (Genesis 24:10–20). When he arrived at the city of Nahor, he had his ten camels kneel down outside the city before the well at the time the women go out to draw water. The servant prayed that the bride-to-be would be evidenced by the fact that she would have consideration for the camels. When Rebekah saw the camels, she *ran* to the well to get water for them.

God the Father sent His Servant the Holy Spirit to search for a bride for His only begotten Son. He has chosen the Ten Commandments to carry this special message from His Lord.

While we may not be able to clearly distinguish the Bride of Christ from the rest of this world, the Holy Spirit knows that the primary reason she draws water from the Well of Salvation is to satisfy the ten thirsting camels of a holy and just Law. The true convert comes to the Savior simply to satisfy the demands of a holy Law. The espoused virgin has respect for the Commandments of God. She is not a worker of lawlessness. Like Paul, she delights in the Law, and says with the psalmist, "I will run in the way of Your commandments" (Psalm 119:32).

The Law is like Aaron's rod that budded (Numbers 17). It looks like hard and dead wood, but from it issues the life of the gospel. If you are not sure if the use of the Law is right, incorporate it into your tabernacle of witness and see if it buds.

When fiery serpents were sent among Israel, they caused the Israelites to admit they had sinned. The serpents also caused them to look up to a bronze serpent that Moses had placed on a pole. That was the means of their salvation. Those who had been bitten and were doomed to die could look at the bronze serpent and live (Numbers 21:6–9). In John 3:14, Jesus specifically cited this Old Testament passage in reference to salvation from sin. The Ten Commandments are like ten biting serpents that carry with them the venomous curse of the Law. It drives sinners to look to the One lifted up on a cross. It was the Law of Moses that put Jesus on the Cross. The Messiah became a curse for us, and redeemed us from the curse of the Law.

> "It is the symptom of an ignorant ministry, and unhealthy state of religion, when the Law is reckoned unimportant."

Jesus rebuked the lawyers because, by their tradition, they had rendered God's Law ineffectual. They even hindered others from entering God's kingdom. This is what Jesus said to them: "Woe to you lawyers! For you have taken away the key of knowledge. You did not enter in yourselves, and those who were entering in you hindered" (Luke 11:52).

The lawyers were professing experts in God's Law. But because they didn't use the "key of knowledge" to bring sinners to the Savior, they hindered its work.

Run to the Border

It must have been incredible to have been alive when Jesus walked on this earth. Sometimes the crowds were so vast that He was forced out into open spaces, or had to minister from a boat pushed out from the shore. On one of these occasions when multitudes crowded Him, there was a woman who had suffered with bleeding for many years. She approached Him from behind, touched the border of His garment, and was immediately healed (Luke 8:43–48).

The world could offer her nothing. She had spent all her resources on medical bills, and rather than getting better, she grew worse. Her life's blood was draining from her body and there was little she could do about it. According to the Law she had become unclean (Leviticus 15:25), so she had nothing to lose by pushing through the crowd to touch this Man from Nazareth. But she wasn't the only one who pressed in on Him to touch the border of His garment:

> Wherever He entered, into villages, cities, or the country, they laid the sick in the marketplaces, and begged Him that they might just touch the border of His garment. And as many as touched Him were made well (Mark 6:56).

What was so special about the border? One answer could be that those who wanted to touch the border of the garment of Jesus needed to stoop low to do so, signifying the humility needed before we can approach the Savior. Grace is for the humble.

However, if we look at Numbers 15:38–40, we see that the border had great significance because it was there to remind the children of Israel of God's Commandments, and consequently to keep them from idolatry.

This helpless woman reached out her trembling hand and felt the hem of His garment touch her fingers. Suddenly, power flowed through her body. But it was something greater than mere power. It was *virtue*. She was *healed* in more than the normal sense of the word.

This story depicts the conversion of the true believer. Our life's blood was draining from our futile being. The Law convinced us that we were without God, without hope, and without righteousness. We were outcasts, aliens from the commonwealth of Israel. It was the Ten Commandments that showed us that our garments were spotted with the filth of the flesh.

Our only hope was to humbly reach out to the fine linen garments of Jesus Christ, and pray that somehow He could help us. Suddenly, power flowed from His body. *Power* to conquer sin, and *virtue* to cleanse us from every transgression. We were purged from the stain of the filth of the flesh …cleansed, sanctified, washed, purified…made *virgins, as though we had never defiled ourselves through sin in the first place*. Like Ruth, we couldn't meet our Redeemer face-to-face unless we were washed, anointed, and wearing our "best garment."

We are freely given this virtue in the gospel. The Church was made into a Virtuous Woman by the grace of almighty God. This is why I think that the virtuous woman described in Proverbs chapter 31 is a vivid picture of the Bride of Christ. Hidden within her virtues are the works of the true believer.

Discerning the Difference

God's Law prepares the heart of the sinner for the good news of the gospel. Without this preparatory work, his heart is hardened and he therefore becomes a candidate for a false conversion. Now and then we can catch a glimpse of the difference between the true and false converts. In 1 Kings 3:16–28 we read the famous narrative of two women, both claiming to be the mother of one child. Solomon, in his wisdom, commanded that the baby be cut in half and thus revealed the true mother.

Both of these women dwelt in the same house. The true and false converts dwell together in the house of the Lord. Each of them called Solomon "lord." Both the true and false convert call Jesus "Lord," and it therefore takes the wisdom of Solomon to discern between the true and false convert. What was it that showed Solomon the real mother? It was that the true mother revealed true love. She would rather lose her child than see him cut in two with a sword.

Here is how to tell the true convert from the false. The spurious convert will reveal himself by dividing the Body of Christ in two with some pet doctrine, rather than backing down in humility. He will cut a body of believers in half because of a particular interpretation of Scripture. He lacks the wisdom that is peaceable and open to reason. In contrast, the true convert will strive to keep the unity of the body. He will not even put meat to his mouth if it causes his brother to stumble, let alone push a personal interpretation and cause division.

More often than not, though, the false convert isn't clearly evident. Like the twins in the womb of Tamar, one has a scarlet thread bound around his hand (Genesis 38:27,28). We may not be able to see who has the scarlet thread of the Blood of Christ bound around his hand, but God can. He knows those who are His. It is the Blood that separates the true from the false.

There are, however, many people who seem to stand as testimonies of modern preaching. They more than likely came into the Church under the message of those who do not use the Law as a schoolmaster to bring sinners to Christ. All that these people heard was that Jesus died on the cross for their sins, and that they would never find true peace until they found peace with God. They were told that they needed to trust Jesus Christ. If you are wondering how to reconcile this teaching with that fact, stay with me for the next chapter.

CHAPTER 6

The Key Was in the Folding

hose who preach grace alone look to the many thousands who have remained in fellowship as clear evidence to justify the presentation of a gospel which makes no reference to the Law.

During a great war, there was a man who invented a parachute that was one hundred percent trustworthy. It made no difference whether the user was large or small; it opened *every* time and got him safely to the ground. The key was in the way it was folded. Every part of the parachute had to be carefully and painstakingly placed in certain positions, following the instructions given by the manufacturer. True, it was somewhat arduous, but it was well worth the effort. It had the effect of ensuring that the life of every precious human being who trusted the parachute would be preserved.

Many years after the war began, a group of young men known as "fast-folders" entered the packing room. These men so influenced the workers with their new fast and easy method of folding that soon they all completely ignored the instruction book given by the manufacturer. Production increased greatly and everyone rejoiced that so much time and effort had been saved.

However, as time passed it slowly became evident that something was radically wrong. In fact, a small group of investigators who went to where the parachutes were being used found to their horror that *of every ten who jumped using the new method, nine tragically fell to their deaths!*

The horrible sight of so many mangled and rotting bodies strewn all over the ground sickened them. These weren't just faceless customers. These were husbands, wives, fathers, mothers, sons, and daughters—cherished human beings who plunged to a needless and terrifying death.

A report was quickly taken back to the fast-folders. Many were heartbroken, and immediately went back to the instruction book and corrected their mistake. With great sobriety and care, they began painstakingly folding each parachute exactly as the book instructed. Their knowledge of the tragedies motivated them to make sure that they did their job with uncompromising conviction.

Yet, there was resistance from a few. Even though they knew that so many lives were being lost, they still refused to follow the instruction book. Unbelievably, they ignored the mass of mangled and rotting bodies, for which they were directly responsible. *Instead, they pointed to those who had survived their fast-folding method as justification for their technique.*

Free From Their Blood

Since the Fall of man, there has been a great battle for the souls of men and women. Those who have gone before us in past centuries have not had an easy task. Labor in the gospel was often slow and arduous. But they knew if they followed *according to the pattern of God's Word*, with His help, they would eventually deliver sinners from death and hell. If they sowed in tears, they would reap in joy. They wanted, above all things, to be "true and faithful witnesses." If they preached the whole counsel of God, they would be free from the blood of all men. These ministries, of men such as Wesley, Wycliff, Whitefield, Spurgeon, and many others, were greatly effective in reaching the lost. *The key was in the careful and thorough use of the Law to prepare the way for the gospel.*

As time went by, certain men discovered that the message of the gospel could be condensed and presented in a much faster and easier way. Unfortunately, this quick and easy method had a number of problems.

First, its presentation was unbiblical. It didn't follow the scriptural example of presenting the balance of Law and grace, as Jesus did. He always preached Law to the proud and arrogant, and grace to the meek and the humble (Luke 10:25,26; 18:18–20; John 3:1–17). Never once did the Son of God give the Good News (the cross, grace, and mercy) to the proud, the arrogant, or the self-righteous. He followed His Father's example: He resists the proud and gives grace to the humble (James 4:6). Paul did the same, as seen at Athens when he used the essence of the First and Second Commandments to reprove their idolatry, and on other occasions (Romans 2:22). Biblical evangelism is *always* Law to the proud and grace to the humble. With the Law, we should break the hard heart, and with the gospel, heal the broken heart. Martin Luther, commenting on **Never once did the Son of God give the Good News to the proud, the arrogant, or the self-righteous.** the right use of the Law, said, "Wherefore this is the proper and absolute use of the Law, by lightning, by tempest and by the sound of the trumpet (as in Mount Sinai) to terrify, and by thundering to beat down and rend in pieces that beast which is called the opinion of righteousness."

Without the Law, there can be no knowledge of sin: "What shall we say then? Is the law sin? Certainly not! On the contrary, *I would not have known sin except through the Law*...For apart from the law sin was dead. I was alive once without the Law, but when the Commandment came, sin revived and I died" (Romans 7:7–9, italics added).

The Law was the instrument of the death of the old nature. It made sure that sinners were truly born again, that the Adamic nature was dealt with by nailing it to the cross. It made certain that the convert was a new creature in Christ.

According to Romans 7:7, the Law of God—specifically the Ten Commandments—is the biblical means of awakening sinners. John Wesley said, "The very first end of the Law, namely, the convicting men of sin; the awakening those who are still asleep on the brink of hell... The ordinary method of God is to convict sinners by the Law, and that only. The gospel is not the means which God hath ordained, or which our Lord Himself used, for this end."

A. W. Pink said,

> The unsaved are in no condition today for the gospel till the Law be applied to their hearts, for "by the Law is the knowledge of sin." It is a waste of time to sow seed on ground which has never been ploughed or spaded! To present the vicarious sacrifice of Christ to those whose dominant passion is to take fill of sin is to give that which is holy to the dogs.

Charles Spurgeon, in speaking of preparing the soil of the heart with the plow of the Law, stated:

> One other reason why this soil was so uncongenial was that it was totally unprepared for the seed. There had been no plowing before the seed was sown, and no harrowing afterwards. He that sows without a plow may reap without a sickle. He who preaches the gospel without preaching the Law may hold all the results of it in his hand, and there will be little for him to hold.

> Robbie Flockhart, when he preached in the streets of Edinburgh, used to say, "You must preach the Law, for the gospel is a silken thread, and you cannot get it into the hearts of men unless you have made a way for it with a sharp needle; the sharp needle of the Law will pull the silken thread of the gospel after it." There must be plow-

ing before there is sowing if there is to be reaping after the sowing.

To what was Jesus referring when He said not to give what is holy to the dogs? To what was He pointing when He said not to cast pearls before swine, lest they trample them under their feet, and turn and tear you in pieces (Matthew 7:6)? The most precious pearl the Church has is "Christ crucified." Preach grace to the proud and watch what they do with it. They will trample the blood of the Savior under their feet with their false profession, and, what's more, they will become enemies of the gospel. If not physically, you can be sure they will tear you in pieces verbally. They have "insulted the Spirit of grace" (Hebrews 10:29). That means they insult the Holy Spirit. "Bitterness" and "backslider" are bad bedfellows for the Church. The proselyte becomes a twofold child of hell.

Those who make a profession of faith without having a humble heart (which the Law produces) have the experience described in 2 Peter 2:22: "According to the true proverb: 'A dog returns to his own vomit,' and 'a sow, having washed, to her wallowing in the mire.'" This is the tragic result of casting pearls of the gospel of grace to the proud, or what the Bible calls "dogs" and "swine."

The false convert has never "crucified the flesh with its passions and desires" (Galatians 5:24). He, like the pig, must go back to wallowing in the mire. Pigs *need* to wallow in mire because they crave the slime to cool their flesh. So it is with the false convert. He never repented, so his flesh is not dead with Christ. It is instead burning with unlawful desire. The heat of lust is too much for his sinful heart; he must go back to the filth.

Yet, the new and modern method of evangelism forsook the Law in its power to humble the proud heart and convert the soul. It did, however, speed the process of evangelism, making it much easier to get commitments. Also, it stirred less opposition and it seemed to get results. So everyone rejoiced.

Second, it failed to mention the fact of Judgment Day. The Bible presents the great and terrible Day of the Lord as *the very reason* to repent and trust the Savior: "Truly, these times of ignorance God overlooked, but now commands all men everywhere to repent, *because He has appointed a day on which He will judge the world in righteousness*" (Acts 17:31, italics added). The new presentation was not faithful to God—it didn't even hint of Judgment Day's approach. The reason Jesus died on the cross was to save us from the wrath to come (1 Thessalonians 1:10). That is the essence of the message of the gospel, but there wasn't even a mention of hell's existence. The "fast-folders" ripped the heart out of the body of the gospel. General William Booth, founder of the Salvation Army, warned that in the twentieth century a gospel would be preached which promised heaven without mentioning hell. Modern evangelism did just that. Take the time to study closely the contents of today's popular tracts and see the flaws of the fast-folding presentation:

1. No mention of Judgment Day.

2. Not a hint of hell.

3. No use of the Law of God to bring the knowledge of personal sin.

4. The gospel is held up as a means of happiness, rather than a means of righteousness.

That is a perfect recipe for a false conversion—a stony-ground hearer. He receives the Word with joy and gladness, but in a time of tribulation, temptation, or persecution, falls away. He is like the "young man" in Mark 14:51,52, who had a "linen cloth thrown around his naked body." When persecution came, he cast off his covering and fled naked.

False converts are nothing new. George Whitefield said of his day, "That is the reason we have so many 'mushroom' converts, because their stony ground is not plowed up; they have not got a conviction of the Law; they are stony-ground hearers."

Charles Finney[1] said, "Evermore the Law *must* prepare the way for the gospel. To overlook this in instructing souls is almost certain to result in false hope, the introduction of a false standard of Christian experience, and to fill the Church with false converts...Time will make this plain."

God knows that I hesitate to be critical of the authors of modern evangelistic literature. They are sincere, earnest, loving, godly brethren, but their zeal for the lost has lacked knowledge of the use of God's Law, and the results are a devastation that cannot be ignored.

After discovering the rampant hypocrisy among professing believers, the author of the most popular of the "God Loves You and Has a Wonderful Plan for Your Life" tracts, said, "A belief that Christians are entitled to the 'good life' can result in demoralizing church members. Expecting the Christian's life to be a bed of roses can be very discouraging to a new Christian—and to more mature ones as well—when they are jostled by the storms of life."

In a book by the same godly author, he weeps at the state of the Church, and earnestly pleads with Christians to clean up their lives. He then concludes the publication with two pages devoted to the Ten Commandments.

Third, the modern method also glossed over sin. Probably the mainstay of the mention of sin in modern evangelism is Romans 3:23: "For all have sinned and fall short of the glory of God." On looking at that Scripture, the question I would ask if I were not a Christian is, "What is meant by 'glory'?" Often we hear how the word "sin" was shouted during archery, to let the archer know that the arrow had fallen short of the target. If I have fallen short of a mark, I would at least want to know what and where the target is *to measure how much I have fallen short*, to know whether I should give up or try another shot.

The Greek word used in the text is *doxa*, which literally means "honor, worship, praise." Humanity has fallen short of the honor, worship, and praise of God by failing to give our Creator the honor, the worship, and the praise due to Him. We have failed to love God with all of our heart, mind, soul, and strength, which is the essence of the Law (Mark 12:30). In fact, "all have sinned" comes in the context of Paul saying that the Law has left the whole world guilty before God (Romans 3:19). By calling "sin!" to a sinner, but failing to tell him anything about the mark he is aiming for, is to let him think that he can still give it his best shot. However, to display the Law in front of him is to leave him without hope of ever coming near the mark, so that his only hope will be in the Savior.

Check the Soil

Here is our problem: Up to ninety percent of the evangelistic crop is failing. They wither and die as soon as the sunlight of tribulation, persecution, and temptation shines on them. We encourage them to be watered by the Word. We give them the "fertilizer" of counsel and support. We follow them up thoroughly, but all to no avail.

So, we then need to check the soil. If, before we plant the seed of the gospel, we take the time to thoroughly turn the soil of the heart with the Law, the effect will be the removal of the stones of sin upon repentance.

God has given us insight into the area in which we are planting. The ground of the human heart is very hard. The Scriptures call it a "heart of stone" (Ezekiel 36:26).

I have heard a number of household-name preachers say that it is biblical normality to have seventy-five percent of those coming to Christ fall away. During an altar call,[2] they know that only one in four of those responding to their message will continue in their faith. So, more than likely they are not too alarmed by modern statistics that reveal an eighty- to ninety-percent failure. This thought is based on the Parable of the Sower, which shows that only twenty-five percent of the crop was on good soil (Mark 4:1–20). But I don't think Jesus gave us this parable as a consolation for disappointing evangelistic results. I think He gave it for our instruction.

When we study the parable closely, we see that the good-soil hearer, the *genuine* convert, had some things the other hearers didn't have. He had *understanding* (Matthew 13:23), and he had a *noble and good heart* (Luke 8:15). Does that mean that throughout humanity, there are those who somehow have understanding and a noble and good heart, and we have to keep on sowing until we find them? No, Scripture makes it clear that there is *none* who understands (Romans 3:11), and that the heart of man is not good, but deceitful and desperately wicked (Jeremiah 17:9).

Up to ninety percent of the evangelistic crop is failing...so we need to check the soil.

How then did the genuine convert obtain these necessary virtues? It is clear that something from *outside* his own heart must have given him understanding and brought him to a point of having a noble and good heart. The schoolmaster taught him that his heart was wicked. The Law turned the soil of his heart and exposed the stones of sin. When these were removed through repentance, it left the good soil of understanding and a heart that saw itself in truth.

An old movie showed an officer of the law entering an illegal gambling casino. Look at what the manager asked the lawman: "Are you going to speak to the people *before* you arrest them? They *must* have the law spelled out to them so they will know that what they are doing is wrong." Doesn't that make sense? How on earth are the gamblers going to come peacefully if they don't realize they have broken the law?

Using the fast-folding method of modern evangelism, we will continue to produce stony-ground "converts," with the devastating results revealed in the next chapter.

CHAPTER 7

Mangled Bodies

ome with me now and see a tragic and sobering sight. We will go to the landing ground on which so many have fallen after putting on the Lord Jesus Christ using the fast-folding method:

- In a 1990 crusade in the U.S., 600 decisions were obtained. No doubt there was much rejoicing. However, ninety days later, follow-up workers *couldn't find even one* who was continuing in his or her faith. That crusade created 600 "backsliders," or to be more scriptural, "false converts."

- In 1991 in Cleveland, Ohio, in an "Inner City Outreach," rejoicing no doubt tapered when those who were involved in follow-up once again couldn't find one of the 400 who had made a decision.

- In 1985, a four-day crusade obtained 217 decisions, but according to a member of the organizing committee, ninety-two percent fell away.

- Charles E. Hackett, the Division of Home Missions National Director for the Assemblies of God in the U.S., said, "A soul at the altar does not generate much excitement in some circles because we realize approximately ninety-five out of every hundred will not become integrated into the church. In fact, most of them will not return for a second visit."

- In his book *Today's Evangelism*, Ernest C. Reisinger said of one outreach, "It lasted eight days, and there were sixty-eight supposed conversions." A month later, not one of the "converts" could be found.

- In 1991 in Salt Lake City, organizers of a concert encouraged follow-up. They said, "Less than five percent of those who respond to an altar call during a public crusade...are living a Christian life one year later." In other words, *more than ninety-five percent* proved to be false converts.

- A pastor in Boulder, Colorado, sent a team to Russia in 1991 and attained 2,500 decisions. The next year, they found that only 30 were going on in their faith. That's a little more than a one-percent retention rate.

- In Leeds, England, a visiting U.S. speaker acquired 400 decisions for a local church. However, six weeks later only two were going on, and they eventually fell away.

- A mass crusade reported 18,000 decisions, yet according to *Church Growth* magazine, tragically ninety-four percent failed to even become incorporated into a local church.

- In November 1970, a number of churches combined for a convention in Fort Worth, Texas, and secured 30,000 decisions. Six months later, the follow-up committee could find only 30 going on in their faith.

- In 1994 in Sacramento, California, a combined crusade yielded over 2,000 commitments. One church followed up 52 of those decisions and couldn't find one conversion.

- In August 1996, a leading U.S. denomination published that during 1995 they secured 384,057 decisions, but retained only 22,983 in fellowship. They couldn't account for 361,074 supposed conversions.

That's a ninety-four percent fall-away rate.

- In Omaha, Nebraska, a pastor of a large church said he was involved with a crusade where 1,300 decisions were made, and not even one "convert" continued in his or her faith.

- Pastor Dennis Grenell from Auckland, New Zealand, who has traveled to India every year since 1980, reported that he saw 80,000 decision cards stacked in a hut in the city of Rajamundry, the "results" of past evangelistic crusades. But he maintained that one would be fortunate to find even 80 Christians in the entire city.

- In the March/April editorial of *American Horizon*, the National Director of Home Missions of a major U.S. denomination disclosed the fact that in 1991, 11,500 churches had obtained 294,784 decisions for Christ. Unfortunately, they could find only 14,337 in fellowship. That means that (no doubt despite the usual intense follow-up) they couldn't account for approximately 280,000 of their decisions.

- A major Christian television network broadcast an interview with a Russian Christian leader on July 5, 1996. She said of Russian converts, "Many thousands have received salvation and healing...but because of there not being many leaders, not many stayed with their faith."

Notice where the blame is laid with the Russian professions of faith. They fell away because they needed more leaders. In light of the fact that God "is able to keep you from falling, and to present you faultless before the presence of His glory with exceeding joy" (Jude 24, KJV), either He *wasn't* able to keep them, or His hand wasn't in their profession of faith in the first place.

Statistics such as the preceding are very hard to find. What organizing committee is going to shout from the housetops that after a mass of pre-crusade prayer, hundreds of thousands of dollars of expenditure, truckloads of follow-up, and the use of a big-name evangelist, initial wonderful results have all but disappeared? Not only would such news be utterly disheartening for all who put so much time and effort into the crusade, *but the committee has no reasonable explanation as to why the massive catch has disappeared.* The statistics are therefore swept under the hushed carpet of discretion.

A Southern California newspaper bravely printed the following article in July 1993:

> "Crusades don't do as much for nonbelievers as some might think," said Peter Wagner, professor of church growth at Fuller Theological Seminary in Pasadena. Three percent to sixteen percent of those who make decisions at crusades end up responsible members of a church, he said. "That's not counting Christians who recommit their lives."

These statistics of an eighty-four to ninety-seven percent fall-away rate are not confined to crusades, but are general throughout local church evangelism. In his book *Fresh Wind, Fresh Fire,* Jim Cymbala notes the lack of growth in the Church: "Despite all the Christian broadcasting and high-profile campaigns, the Christian population is not growing in numbers nationally. In fact, church attendance in a given week during 1996 was down to 37 percent of the population, a ten-year low...even though 82 percent of Americans claim to be Christians" (Zondervan, p. 90). The problem is not with the crusades, but with the methods and message of modern evangelism.

Sadly, these are not isolated cases. The mangled bodies of those who are erroneously called "backsliders" lay strewn on the ground as a disastrous result of a fast-folded gospel.

I received the following letter from a pastor in Florida:

> We have seen...over a thousand led to the Lord on the streets...Not many of these teens are at church. I've been analyzing this, and last month, for example, I preached face to face on the streets the whole gospel (death, burial, and resurrection) with a focus on repentance and remission to 155 people. Seventy made commitments to Christ. I know my preaching is correct, but I know I need better follow-up; any recommendations?

His dilemma was that he was preaching the light of the gospel (Christ's death, burial, and resurrection) without using the Law to awaken his hearers. Like many others who see this enigma, he thought that his converts needed more follow-up. A respected minister, whose evangelism program has exploded across the world, said that his policy attempts to get at the heart of the fall-away rate of new converts "by placing great stress on the follow-up." However, to fall into the trap of thinking that follow-up is the answer is like supposing that putting a stillborn child into intensive care will solve the problem.

Gordon Miller wrote an article in which he addresses the converts who stay in the Church—the "sinning converts" issue. He said,

> A few months ago, a senior minister of a large growing church rang me about a new situation in their church ...An increasing number of converts bring their old ways into their Christian lives and do things that shock their leaders. Here, after further reflection, is an extended version of my response.
>
> The first thing to note is that this church and its ministers haven't diluted the gospel or lowered their standards. The church is one of the best in the country with gifted, godly leaders. They fearlessly preach a no-compromise gospel and are even better at nurture than they

were years ago. Yet an increasing number of their numerous converts fail to show evidence of moral change in their lives.

Again, even a "no-compromise gospel" will not awaken sinners. That's not its function. Author and Bible teacher Paris Reidhead, in remarking about the ministry of Charles Finney, wrote:

> Finney was in Rochester, New York, where a blue-ribbon committee of outstanding citizens was appointed by Henry Ward Beecher to study the converts who, a decade earlier, had come to Christ under Finney's preaching. It was found that eighty-five percent of those who had made professions of faith under Finney's preaching were still faithfully living for Christ.
>
> In contrast, it is being reported that only one-half of one percent of those who make decisions for Christ in our evangelistic meetings today will be living as Christians two years from now. This should give you some idea of how far we've strayed from the Word of God (*Finding the Reality of God*).[3]

Perhaps you are thinking, "But I didn't have the Law preached to me when I came to Christ." Let me ask you a few questions. When you came to the Savior, did you have a knowledge of sin? You must have, or you would not have repented. He who repents turns from sin, and "sin" is transgression of the Law (1 John 3:4).

What then was your sin? Was it lust, adultery, or fornication? If so, then your sin was that you transgressed the 7th Commandment. Did you steal (8th), hate (6th), lie (9th), or blaspheme (3rd)? Were you covetous (10th)? Were you selfish or ungrateful to God? Did you realize that God should be first in your life (1st, 4th)? Or maybe you suddenly discerned that God was nothing like you thought He was (2nd). Did you feel bad about your attitude toward your parents

(5th)? How did you know that you had sinned against God? Wasn't it because you knew of the Ten Commandments? Someone, somewhere, somehow had said to you: "You shall not kill, you shall not steal," etc., and your conscience bore witness with the Law. Like Paul, you too can say, "I would not have known sin except through the Law" (Romans 7:7).

Impersonal Statistics

On a Saturday sometime in 1998 near Davis, California, a female student from Sacramento and a skydiving instructor (who had made about two thousand jumps) leaped from a plane at ten thousand feet. Both were in their twenties. Tragically their parachute failed to open and their reserve became tangled in the main chute. Witnesses said that they heard the young woman screaming for help, *and felt the impact about two football fields away*. It was the woman's first jump. Needless to say, it was her and her instructor's last.

We can lose sight of the reality that we are speaking about the salvation of individual human beings.

I have related this true story to bring a *personal* note to the horror of seeing someone entrust her life to a parachute, and having it fail. One would never forget the sound of a terrified young lady screaming, nor the experience of feeling the earth shake as her fragile body hit the ground. The cold statistic that one in a hundred thousand jumps ends in death somehow loses its reality, but (depending on your tenderness of heart) the details of one young woman's death is heartrending. In the same way, we can speak about how many hundreds of thousands fall away from the faith, and lose sight of the reality that we are speaking about the salvation of *individual* human beings.

I can't put into words the heartbreak of seeing so many spurious converts who have left the Church, and the multitudes of false converts who stay *within* the Church. A. W. Tozer wrote, "It is my opinion that tens of thousands of people, if not millions, have been brought into some kind of religious experience by accepting Christ, and they have not been saved."

We are not talking about mere statistics, but the salvation of human beings from death and eternal damnation in hell. We must put a quick end to the fast and easy method, even though it eliminates the reproach of the gospel and *seems* to be filling our churches.

Please, don't be tempted to ignore the devastating results of modern evangelism, and to look at those *comparatively* few who are continuing in their faith as justification for the method. Remember, for every 1,000 genuine converts, there are as many as 9,000 who lay mangled on the soil of hard hearts, as a direct result of the quick and easy methods of modern evangelism.

CHAPTER 8

Making Grace Amazing

*A*n editorial, after reporting that 280,000 converts couldn't be accounted for, concluded by saying, "Something is wrong." It has been wrong for nearly one hundred years of evangelism, since the Church forsook the key to the sinner's heart. As we have seen, when it set aside the Law of God in its function to convert the soul (Psalm 19:7), the Church removed the sinner's means of seeing his need of God's forgiveness.

Romans 5:20 tells us why God's Law entered the scene: "Moreover the law entered that the offense might abound. But where sin abounded, grace abounded much more." When sin abounds, grace abounds "much more"; and according to Scripture, the thing that makes sin abound is the Law.

We can see the work of God's Law illustrated in civil law. Watch what often happens on a freeway when there is no visible sign of the law. See how motorists transgress the speed limit. It would seem that each speedster says to himself that the law has forgotten to patrol his part of the freeway. He is transgressing the law by only 15 mph, and besides, he isn't the only one doing it.

Notice what happens when the law enters the fast lane, with red lights flashing. The speeder's heart misses a beat. He is no longer secure in the fact that other motorists are also speeding. He knows that he is *personally* as guilty as the next guy, and *he* could be the one the law pulls over. Suddenly, his "mere" 15 mph transgression doesn't seem such a small thing after all; it seems to abound.

Look at the freeway of sin. The whole world naturally goes with the flow. Who hasn't had an "affair" (or desired to) at some time or another? Who in today's society doesn't tell the occasional "white" lie? Who doesn't take something that belongs to someone else, even if it's just "white-collar" crime? They know they are doing wrong, but their security is in the fact that so many others are just as guilty, if not more so. It seems God has forgotten all about sin and the Ten Commandments—the wicked "has said in his heart, 'God has forgotten; He hides His face; He will never see it'" (Psalm 10:11).

Now watch the Law enter with red lights flashing. The sinner's heart is stopped. He places his hand on his mouth. He examines the speedometer of his conscience. Suddenly, it shows him the measure of his guilt in a new light—the light of the Law. His sense of security in the fact that there are multitudes doing the same thing becomes irrelevant, because every man will give an account of *himself* to God. Sin not only becomes personal, it seems to "abound." His mere lust becomes *adultery of the heart* (Matthew 5:27,28), his white lie, *false witness*; his own way becomes *rebellion*; his hatred, *murder* (1 John 3:15); his "sticky" fingers make him a thief—"Moreover the law entered that the offense might abound." Without the Law entering, sin is neither personal, nor is it veritable: "For without the Law sin is dead [the sense of it is inactive and a lifeless thing]" (Romans 7:8, Amplified).

It was the Commandment that showed Paul sin in its true light, that it is "exceedingly sinful" (Romans 7:13). Paul spoke from his own experience because he sat at the feet of Gamaliel, the great teacher of the Law, and therefore saw sin in its vivid colors.

The Offense and the Foolishness of the Cross

According to the Scriptures, "[the real function of] the Law is to make men recognize and be conscious of sin [not mere perception, but an acquaintance with sin which works toward repentance...]" (Romans 3:20, Amplified).

To illustrate this point, imagine if I said to you, "I have some good news for you. *Someone has just paid a $25,000 speeding fine on your behalf!*" You would probably answer me with some cynicism in your voice, "What are you talking about? I *don't have* a $25,000 speeding fine!" Your reaction would be quite understandable. If you don't know that you have broken the law in the first place, the good news of someone paying a fine for you won't be good news; it will be foolishness to you. My insinuation of unlawful activity will even be offensive to you.

But if I were to put it this way it may make more sense: "Today, the law clocked you traveling at 55 mph in an area designated for a blind children's convention. You totally ignored ten clear warning signs saying that the maximum speed was 15 mph. What you did was *extremely* dangerous. The fine is $25,000 or imprisonment. The law was about to take its course when someone you don't even know stepped in and paid the fine for you. *You are very fortunate.*"

Can you see that telling you the good news of the fine being paid, without telling you that you have broken the law first, will leave you thinking the "good news" is nothing but nonsense? However, clearly making known your transgression gives *sense* to the good news. An unclouded explanation of the law, *so that you can plainly see your violation*, helps you understand and appreciate the good news.

In the same way, telling someone the good news that Jesus died on the cross for his sins makes no sense to him: "For the message of the cross is foolishness to those who are perishing" (1 Corinthians 1:18). Therefore it is also quite understandable for him to say, "What are you talking about?

I haven't got any 'sins.' I try to live a good life," etc. Your insinuation that he is a sinner, when he doesn't think he is, will be offensive to him.

But those who take the time to follow in the footsteps of Jesus and open up the spirituality of the Law, carefully explaining the meaning of the Ten Commandments, will see the sinner become *convicted by the Law as a transgressor* (James 2:9). Once he understands his transgression, the good news will be neither offensive nor foolishness, but the power of God to salvation.

What 'Sin' Are You Talking About?

When David sinned with Bathsheba, he broke *all* of the Ten Commandments. He coveted his neighbor's wife, lived a lie, stole her, committed adultery, murdered her husband, dishonored his parents, and thus broke the remaining four commandments in reference to his relationship with God. So, the Lord sent Nathan the prophet to reprove him (2 Samuel 12:1–13).

There is great significance in the order in which the reproof came. Nathan gave David (the shepherd of Israel) a parable about something that he could understand—sheep. He began with the natural realm, rather than immediately exposing the king's sin. He told a story about a rich man who, instead of taking a sheep from his own flock, killed a poor man's pet lamb to feed a stranger.

David was indignant, and sat up on his high throne of self-righteousness. He revealed his knowledge of the Law by saying that the guilty party would restore fourfold and would die for his crime. Nathan then exposed the king's sin of taking another man's "lamb," saying, "You are the man!...Why have you despised the commandment of the Lord, to do evil in His sight?" When David cried, "I have sinned against the Lord!", the prophet *then* gave him grace and said, "The Lord also has put away your sin; you shall not die."

Imagine if Nathan, *fearful of rejection*, changed things around a little, and instead told David, "God loves you and has a wonderful plan for your life. However, there is something which is keeping you from enjoying this wonderful plan; it is called 'sin.'"

Imagine if he had glossed over the *personal nature* of David's sin, with a general reference to *all* men having sinned and fallen short of the glory of God. David's reaction may have been, "What *sin* are you talking about?" rather than to admit his terrible transgression. Think of it—why should he cry, *"I have sinned against the Lord!"* at the sound of *that* message? Instead, he may have, in a sincere desire to experience this "wonderful plan," admitted that he, like all men, had sinned and fallen short of the glory of God.

If David had not been made to *tremble* under the wrath of the Law, the prophet would have removed the very means of producing godly sorrow, which was so necessary for David's repentance. It is "godly sorrow" that produces repentance (2 Corinthians 7:10). It was the weight of his guilt that caused him to cry out, *"I have sinned against the Lord!"* The Law caused him to labor and become heavy laden; it made him hunger and thirst for righteousness. It enlightened him as to the *serious* nature of sin as far as God was concerned.

We received the following letter from someone who had listened to our teaching online and then tried using the Law in his preaching. He wrote: "I visited the Lebanon, Tennessee, prison system and witnessed to around thirty hardcore criminals in the maximum security area. I have never seen grown men cry like that!"

This letter came from Colorado: "God introduced me to your [teaching].[4] New power and anointing came my way and in preaching the Law over the last nine months or so, I have seen the fruit falling! Grown men crying, teens falling to their knees in front of their peers, and skeptics taking a new look."

Sin is like an onion. Its outer wrapper is a dry and crusty self-righteousness. It is only when its external casing is peeled away that it brings tears to the human eye. The Law peels the onion and allows contrition.

The Vase

A child broke his father's antique vase. It was one that he was forbidden to touch, worth $25,000. However, the child thought the vase was merely worth $2, so he wasn't too concerned. He could easily replace it. It was only when he was later told of its true value that he saw the seriousness of his transgression and felt sorrow of heart. It was knowledge of the solemn nature of breaking an expensive antique, which he had been told not to touch, that enabled him to feel sorrow. If he had been left in ignorance of the value of the vase, he wouldn't have been truly sorry. Would you be upset if you had broken a vase you could easily replace?

The Law-less "God loves you" message doesn't show the sinner the utterly serious nature of his transgression.

The Law-less "God loves you and has a wonderful plan for your life" message doesn't cause the sinner to tremble. It doesn't show him the utterly serious nature of his transgression, so he doesn't find godly sorrow that produces repentance.

How true are these words spoken by Charles Spurgeon, the Prince of Preachers: "The Law serves a most necessary purpose." He also said of sinners, "They will *never* accept grace, until they tremble before a just and holy Law." Those who see the role of the Law will be Sons of Thunder *before* they are the Sons of Consolation. They know that the shoes of human pride must be removed before sinners can approach the burning bush of the gospel.

It is important to realize that we *can* evoke a tearful response from sinners by telling them that God loves them. The message is more appealing to both the Christian and the sinner. It is certainly *easier* to speak of love than to speak of sin. Many years ago, before I understood the function of God's Law, I told a prostitute of God's love and was delighted that she immediately began weeping. Unbeknown to me, her tears were not tears of godly sorrow for sin, but merely an emotional response to the need of a father's love. In my ignorance, I joyfully led her in a sinner's prayer. However, I was disappointed some time later when she fell away, and her tender heart became *very* calloused toward the things of God.

Paradoxical as it may seem, the Law makes grace abound, in the same way darkness makes light shine. It was John Newton, the writer of "Amazing Grace," who said that a wrong understanding of the harmony between Law and grace would produce "error on the left and the right hand." I don't know if any of us could claim to have a better understanding of grace than the one who penned such a hymn.

The question arises, Should a sinner be moved by Law or grace, by fear or love, when it comes to his salvation? We'll look at this in the next chapter.

CHAPTER 9

From What Did They Flee?

*I*n 1993, the Washington, D.C. traffic authorities found themselves in a public dilemma. Members of a foreign embassy had been issued numerous parking tickets for breaking the law, but because their status made them immune to any form of prosecution, they therefore felt no obligation to pay for their violations. To that date, *they owed the city six million dollars in unpaid fines.*

What happened? They simply had no respect for the law, or for the agency of the law, *because there was no fear of future punishment.* They consequently became bold in their lawlessness.

However, in an effort to force them to pay their debts, authorities came up with a scheme where vehicles that were driven by traffic violators would not be able to be registered, so violators would therefore be unable to drive their cars.

The same thing has happened with the Church. It has failed to preach future punishment for violation of God's Law. Therefore sinners have become bold in their lawlessness. They have lost respect both for the Law and for its agency, the Church.

In San Diego, a strip club has a large sign that reads "We didn't create sin, we just perfected it." One TV channel boasted of their adult programming: "Guaranteed to break more Commandments than any other lineup." A magazine cover in the Los Angeles Airport was headlined "Teenage Sex Romps. Stuff so bad, it's good. We're *so* ashamed." The secular world has become devoid of the fear of God; but how can they be expected to fear the Lord when much of the Church is offended by the doctrine? Unbeknown to them, they are daily clocking up debt to the Law, thinking that they will never have to pay the bill. They are storing up wrath that will be revealed in the Day of Wrath (Romans 2:5). If on that Day they are found in debt, they will pay for it with their souls. There will be hell to pay. Unless they are *convinced* that the Day of Reckoning is coming, that God will bring to judgment every secret thing, whether it is good or evil, they will continue to believe that God does not require an account.

Not Moved by Fear

L. E. Maxwell, Bible teacher and principal at the Prairie Bible Institute in Alberta, Canada, wrote of how students came to a knowledge of salvation. Some were "moved by fear" and others were "moved by love." He noted that between 1931 and 1949, of the 2,507 students, nearly sixty-five percent were moved by fear, and only six percent were moved by love. The remaining twenty-nine percent came with another motive or couldn't remember why they came to the Savior.

This side of Judgment Day, one can only surmise as to *how* those not moved by fear ever found a place of repentance. This thought provokes the following inquiries:

- When they found a place of repentance, of what did they repent? It *must* have been "sin."

- When they understood that they had *sinned against God*, did they not fear at all? Didn't they have reverence enough for God to produce the fear of the Lord, which is the beginning of wisdom?

- When they turned from sin, how did they "flee from the wrath to come" without fear?

- If they were "moved by the love of God" seen in the cross, did they not fear at the extreme to which God went to redeem them because of their sin?

As Christians, have they yet come to a point of fearing God? What do they think when they read that God killed a husband and wife because they broke the Ninth Commandment (Acts 5:1–10)? Do they conclude that the psalmist was misguided when he wrote, "My flesh trembles for fear of You, and I am afraid of Your judgments" (Psalm 119:120)? Have they obeyed the command of Jesus: "I will show you whom you should fear: Fear Him who, after He has killed, has power to cast into hell; yes, I say to you, fear Him!" (Luke 12:5)? Psalm 2:11 commands, "Serve the Lord with fear, and rejoice with trembling." The early Church did just that; they walked "in the fear of the Lord" (Acts 9:31). Do they have Paul's motive for seeking the lost: "Knowing, therefore, the terror of the Lord, we persuade men" (2 Corinthians 5:11)?

Scripture makes it very clear what it is that causes men to flee from sin. It's the "fear of the Lord" (Proverbs 16:6). Understandably, Maxwell's conclusion was not a concern that so many had fled to Christ in fear, *but that some hadn't.* When F. B. Meyer questioned 400 Christian workers about why they came to Christ, "an overwhelming number testified that it was because of some message or influence of the terror of the Lord." The famous Bible teacher then said, "Oh, this is more than interesting and astonishing, especially in these days when we are rebuked often for not preaching more of the love of God!" R. C. Sproul said, "Jesus doesn't save us *to* God. He saves us *from* God." He also stated, "There's probably no concept in theology more repugnant to modern America than the idea of divine wrath."

Well-versed

As I was waiting to witness to a couple, I couldn't help but hear some of the filthy language a young lady was using to describe a situation that displeased her. When I found a gap in the conversation, I gave them a couple of our tracts, along with two pennies with the Ten Commandments pressed into them, and swung the conversation to the Law. The young lady with the dirty mouth claimed she was a Christian, but when I said that I had heard her language and that something wasn't right, she admitted she was a "backslider." She was very well versed in the knowledge of the way of salvation, but she was adamant that one should not come to Christ because of the fear of "Judgment Day, hell, or the wrath of God." She said that we should come to Christ because of God's love, expressed in the cross.

It was obvious by her sinful lifestyle that she had mere head knowledge of God's love. She didn't consider it a love worthy of her attention. When I told her, "Jesus said, 'Don't fear him who has power to kill your body, and afterward can do no more. But fear Him who has power to kill the body and cast your soul into hell; fear Him,' then she said, "I think that you were *sent* to me today."

A. W. Tozer wrote in *The Knowledge of the Holy*:

> God's justice stands forever against the sinner in utter severity. The vague and tenuous hope that God is too kind to punish the ungodly has become a deadly opiate for the consciences of millions. It hushes their fears and allows them to practice all pleasant forms of iniquity while death draws every day nearer and the command to repent goes unregarded. As responsible moral beings, we dare not so trifle with our eternal future.

A close friend of mine told me that as a professing Christian he lacked the fear of God. To him, God was just a good friend. One day he found out that his girlfriend's parents were out of town. He immediately dropped to his knees and earnestly prayed, "Lord, this could be of You. I want to lose my virginity today. I will know it's of You if she says to come on over." She invited him over and he became a fornicator that day. Then he earnestly thanked God for what he saw as the Lord giving him his heart's desire.

He found a place of genuine repentance some time later, and is now soundly saved and fervently serving God.

A lack of the fear of God isn't confined to the pews. Some years ago, *Christianity Today* found (in a confidential survey) that nearly one in four *pastors* in the U.S. had been involved in some sort of sexual sin.

"The vague and tenuous hope that God is too kind to punish the ungodly has become a deadly opiate for millions."

Those who lack the fear of God will not stop at fornication. A wise man once said, "Most I fear God. Next to Him, I fear him that fears Him not." If someone has no fear of God, he will lie to you, steal from you, and even kill you...if he thinks he can get away with it.

How Many Lies?

A six-year-old boy once approached his father, who, as a pastor, understood the importance of a sinner having knowledge of sin. The child said that he wanted to "ask Jesus into his heart." The father, suspecting that the child lacked the knowledge of sin, told him that he could do so when he was older, then sent him off to bed.

A short time later, the boy got out of bed and asked his father if he could give his life to the Savior. The father still wasn't persuaded of the son's understanding, and not wanting the child's salvation to be spurious, he sent him back to his room. A third time the son returned. This time the father questioned him about whether he had broken any of the Ten Commandments. The young boy didn't think he had. When he was asked if he had lied, the child said that he hadn't. The father thought for a moment, then asked him how many lies he had to tell to be a liar. When it was established that one lie made a person a liar, the child realized he had lied, then broke down in uncontrollable tears. When the father then asked him if he wanted to ask Jesus into his heart, the child *cringed* and nodded his head. He was cringing because he now had a knowledge that he had sinned against God. That produced fear. At this point, he could do more than experimentally "ask Jesus into his heart." He could find a place of godly sorrow. Even at his young age, he could exercise repentance toward the God he now understood that he had offended.

After speaking of the importance of the place of fear, L. E. Maxwell said:

> Is the majesty of the Moral Ruler to meet with no respect? Is the authority of His Law of no consequence? Is there nothing in God to fear? An effete dilettantism would feign tell us so. Nevertheless all history and Scripture and experience cry out against such an emasculated and effeminate theology.

It is the fear of God that should stop the Christian from flirting with the eternal well-being of sinners by diluting the message with which he has been entrusted. His devotion to the truth will be rewarded: "Those who rebuke the wicked will have delight, and a good blessing will come upon them" (Proverbs 24:25).

It seems that John Wesley had those in his day who refused to preach the Law to bring the knowledge of sin. They justified their method by saying that they preached "Christ and Him crucified." So Wesley pointed to Paul's method of preaching Christ crucified:

> When Felix sent for Paul, on purpose that he might "hear him concerning the faith in Christ;" instead of preaching Christ in *your* sense (which would probably have caused the Governor, either to mock or to contra-

dict and blaspheme,) "he reasoned of righteousness, temperance, and judgment to come," till Felix (hardened as he was) "trembled," (Acts 24:24,25). Go thou and tread in his steps. Preach Christ to the careless sinner, by reasoning "of righteousness, temperance, and judgment to come!"

The Bible gives us further insight into Paul's reasoning. In Acts 28:23 we read, "When they had appointed him a day, many came to him at his lodging, to whom he explained and solemnly testified of the kingdom of God, persuading them concerning Jesus from both the Law of Moses and the Prophets, from morning till evening."

Our aim in preaching is to persuade sinners "concerning Jesus." *He* is the way, the truth, and the life. Without Him they will perish. How does Paul do that? He used *both* prophecy and the Law of Moses. Prophecy appeals to a man's intellect and creates faith in the Word of God. As he realizes that the Bible is no ordinary book—that it contains numerous indisputable prophecies that substantiate its supernatural origin—he begins to give Scripture credibility. However, the Law of Moses appeals to a man's *conscience* and brings the knowledge of sin. Paul used "both" because prophecy doesn't bring an awareness of sin.

A New Gospel Presentation

A well-known charismatic couple, whose aim is to reach millions with the gospel, say that they have discovered a new method to get people saved. They maintain that an angel told the woman how to get instant decisions. Let's assume that you are in a restaurant and you want a waitress to make a decision for Christ. This is what you would say:

"Do you know there are two kinds of beautiful waitresses?" Their answer: "Really?" Then you say, "Yes! Those who are saved and those who are about to be. Which one are you?" If their answer is anything other than, "I am saved," say, "Repeat this after me: 'Father, forgive my sins. Jesus, come into my heart. Make me the kind of person You want me to be. Thank You for saving me.'" Now, ask the person: "Where is Jesus right now?" If they answer, "In my heart," say, "Congratulations on being a child of God!" If their answer is anything else, have them repeat the prayer after you again.

The couple also insist, "When you talk to someone, use the same words the angel said. It works! If you change the words, it does not work!"

This technique that the "angel" gave the woman isn't new. It is the age-old selling approach of manipulating a customer so that he will answer in the way you want him to. However, there is one important difference. Waitresses are trained to be congenial to customers—not only for the sake of their job, but because the size of their tip depends on it.

Why would an angel of God, after 2,000 years of evangelism, suddenly announce a method that isn't in line with God's revealed Word? Did God suddenly figure out a new way to reach the lost, and then send His angel to tell us? Did He change His mind about how to reach the world?

If an angel from heaven told me of a gospel (or a method of gospel promotion) that wasn't in line with Holy Scripture, I would reject it without a second thought. Why would I do such a thing, even if it *seemed* to work? Simply because I fear God in light of the apostle Paul's sober warning in Galatians 1:8: "But even if we, *or an angel from heaven*, preach any other gospel to you than what we have preached to you, let him be accursed" (italics added).

Again, I cannot express my anguish over this type of "evangelism." My heart's cry is for people to be saved from hell, and yet modern methods work *against*, not *for* that end. Dare I say it, but they are doing the *devil's* work rather than the Lord's. In Matthew 13:25 we are told, "While men slept, his enemy came and sowed tares among the wheat and went his way." As Christians we must be alert to the workings of the enemy, understand about true and false conversions, and fear God enough to follow in the steps of *biblical* evangelism. We should heed Paul's warning against "peddling God's Word [shortchanging and adulterating the divine message]" (2 Corinthians 2:17, Amplified). John Wesley said that those who didn't bother to use the Law were either "babes in Christ, or strangers to regeneration."

A pastor of a large church in the South told me that almost every person in the "Bible Belt" parrots the same phrase. As soon as they are personally challenged about their salvation they say, "I have received Jesus Christ as Lord and Savior. I've dealt with that," and yet he knows in his heart of hearts that there are no signs of regeneration. He said that it's as though they have been inoculated against the truth. *They have.*

I received the following letter from a very concerned mother:

> It was at a youth camp that my oldest son "gave his heart to Jesus" and was baptized, but since then has shown no real desire that I can see to live for the Lord. I don't want to seem critical, but I just don't see the desire in any way, shape, or form. I don't want to see the same thing happen with my other two kids.

God only knows how many others have had the experience of seeing false professions of loved ones. When these false converts fall away, they become bitter, and their latter end becomes *worse* than the first. They are *inoculated* against the truth. What can this mother now say to her son?

I deal with so many who are more than fruitless converts, they are venomous "backsliders." They have enough ammunition to do great damage to the cause of the gospel. Yet, as they pour out their hatred and filthy blasphemy, my heart goes out to them because they are the sad product of manipulative modern methods.

The next time you find someone who is into the occult or some weird cult, dig a little, and then don't be surprised when you find that they once "gave their heart to Jesus." Scripture warns that many false converts will leave the Church: "Now the Spirit expressly says that in latter times *some will depart from the faith,* giving heed to deceiving spirits and doctrines of demons" (1 Timothy 4:1, italics added).

The Driving Power

Charles Spurgeon reiterates the importance of stressing the coming Day of Judgment:

> God [has] appointed a Day in which He will judge the world, and we sigh and cry until it shall end the reign of wickedness, and give rest to the oppressed. Brethren, we must preach the coming of the Lord, and preach it somewhat more than we have done; *because it is the driving power of the gospel.* Too many have kept back these truths, and thus the bone has been taken out of the arm of the gospel. Its point has been broken; its edge has been blunted. The doctrine of judgment to come is the power by which men are to be aroused. There is another life; the Lord will come a second time; judgment will arrive; the wrath of God will be revealed. *Where this is not preached, I am bold to say the gospel is not preached.* It is absolutely necessary to the preaching of the gospel of Christ that men be warned as to what will happen if they continue in their sins.
>
> Ho, ho sir surgeon, you are too delicate to tell the man that he is ill! You hope to heal the sick without their knowing it. You therefore flatter them; and what happens? They laugh at you; they dance upon their own graves. At last they die! Your delicacy is cruelty; your flatteries are poisons; *you are a murderer.* Shall we keep

men in a fool's paradise? Shall we lull them into soft
slumbers from which they will awake in hell? Are we to
become helpers of their damnation by our smooth
speeches? In the name of God we will not.

In *Striking Incidents of Saving Grace*, Henry Breeden tells of
a preacher in Colliery, England, who saw a number of conversions take place under his ministry. Then in 1861 a
"stranger" passed through and conducted meetings in which
"there were great numbers of persons" who professed faith in
Jesus. The preacher then recounts the
sad effects:

> But many of them were, in a short
> time, gone back again into the world.
> Indeed, so complete was the failure
> that the Minister who succeeded me
> in that Circuit said, "There was not
> one single person, out of about nine-
> ty who professed to obtain Religion
> through that man's services, that con-
> tinued to be a member of the Colliery
> Church."

"The wrath of God will be revealed. Where this is not preached, I am bold to say the gospel is not preached."

I had observed the same sort of thing before in regard
to the efforts of suchlike persons in other places. And,
therefore, I was very desirous to find out what was the
cause of such failures. I was sure that the persons, said to
be brought in under my own ministry, had nearly all of
them held on their way, and were then members—either
in the Church above, or in the Church below. So I set
myself calmly to consider the whole affair. In doing this,
I soon found that the preaching that does not address
the sinner's conscience, and strive to break the uncon-
verted spirit down by enforcing the Law of God, scarcely
ever leads to the salvation of the soul. And these men
scarcely ever preach the Law.

Yes, that is it, and nothing else—"By the Law is the

knowledge of sin." Let a minister get that important sentiment burnt into his very soul by the Light and flaming Love of God. And then let him go forth and preach the truth as it is in Jesus, and many, many precious souls will soon be saved. But let him omit preaching the Law, and whatever else he may do—for he can accomplish many great things—yet, under that man's ministry, conversions will be scarce (Harvey Christian Publishers, pp. 188,189).

I couldn't give a more hearty "Amen!" to his conclusion: "Yes, that is it, and nothing else—'By the Law is the knowledge of sin.'" This teaching is so foundational, and yet we have failed to see its simple truth. In the next chapter we are going to look at the importance of a sinner's motive in his response to the gospel.

CHAPTER 10

The Motive and the Result

*L*et me now share with you a portion of a teaching I often give which tends to clarify the motive sinners should have when they come to the Savior.

Two men are seated in a plane. The first is given a parachute and told to put it on, as it would improve his flight. He's a little skeptical at first, since he can't see how wearing a parachute in a plane could possibly improve his flight.

After some time, he decides to experiment and see if the claims are true. As he puts it on, he notices the weight of it upon his shoulders and he finds he has difficulty in sitting upright. However, he consoles himself with the fact that he was told the parachute would improve his flight. So he decides to give it a little time.

As he waits, he notices that some of the other passengers are laughing at him because he's wearing a parachute in a plane. He begins to feel somewhat humiliated. As they continue to laugh and point at him, he can stand it no longer. He sinks in his seat, unstraps the parachute, and throws it to the floor. Disillusionment and bitterness fill his heart, because as far as he was concerned he was told an outright lie.

The second man is given a parachute, *but listen to what he is told.* He's told to put it on because at any moment he'll be jumping 25,000 feet out of the plane. He gratefully puts the parachute on. He doesn't notice the weight of it upon his shoulders, nor that he can't sit upright. His mind is consumed with the thought of what would happen to him if he jumped without the parachute.

Let's now analyze the *motive* and the *result* of each passenger's experience. The first man's motive for putting the parachute on was solely to improve his flight. The result of his experience was that he was humiliated by the passengers, disillusioned, and somewhat embittered against those who gave him the parachute. As far as he's concerned, it will be a long time before anyone gets one of those things on his back again.

The second man put the parachute on solely to escape the jump to come. And because of his knowledge of what would happen to him if he jumped without it, he has a deep-rooted joy and peace in his heart knowing that he's saved from sure death. This knowledge gives him the ability to withstand the mockery of the other passengers. His attitude toward those who gave him the parachute is one of heartfelt gratitude.

If we are true and faithful witnesses, that's what we'll be preaching—that there is wrath to come.

Listen to what the modern gospel says: "Put on the Lord Jesus Christ. He'll give you love, joy, peace, fulfillment, and lasting happiness." In other words, Jesus will improve your flight. The sinner responds, and in an experimental fashion puts on the Savior to see if the claims are true. And what does he get? The promised temptation, tribulation, and persecution—the other passengers mock him. So what does he do? He takes off the Lord Jesus Christ; he's offended for the Word's sake; he's disillusioned and somewhat embittered; and quite rightly so. He was promised peace, joy, love, and fulfillment, and all he got were trials and humiliation. His bitterness is directed toward those who gave him the so-called "good news." His latter end becomes worse than the first—he's another inoculated and bitter "backslider."

Instead of preaching that Jesus improves the flight, we should be warning the passengers that they have to jump out of a plane. That it's appointed for man to die once, and after this the judgment. When a sinner understands the horrific consequences of breaking the Law of God, he will flee to the Savior solely to escape the wrath that's to come. If we are true and faithful witnesses, that's what we'll be preaching— that there is wrath to come—that "God commands all men everywhere to repent, *because* He has appointed a day on which He will judge the world in righteousness." The issue isn't one of happiness, but one of righteousness. The fact that the Bible doesn't mention the word "happiness" even *once*, yet mentions "righteousness" 289 times, should make the issue clear.

It doesn't matter how happy a sinner is, or how much he is enjoying the pleasures of sin for a season; without the righteousness of Christ, he will perish on the day of wrath. The Bible says, "Riches do not profit in the day of wrath, but righteousness delivers from death" (Proverbs 11:4). Peace and joy are legitimate *fruits* of salvation, but it's not legitimate to use these fruits as a drawing card for salvation. If we do so, the sinner will respond with an impure motive, lacking repentance.

Can you remember why the *second* passenger had joy and peace in his heart? It was because he knew that the parachute was going to save him from sure death. In the same way, as believers, we have joy and peace in believing because we know that the righteousness of Christ is going to deliver us from the wrath which is to come.

With that thought in mind, let's take a close look at an incident aboard the plane. We have a brand new flight attendant. It's her first day, and she's carrying a tray of boiling hot coffee. She wants to leave an impression on the passengers and she certainly does! As she's walking down the aisle, she trips over someone's foot and slops the hot coffee all over the lap of our second passenger. What's his reaction as that boiling liquid hits his tender flesh? Does he say, "Man, that hurt!"? Yes, he does. But then does he rip the parachute from his shoulders, throw it to the floor, and say, "That stupid parachute!"? No; why should he? He didn't put the parachute on for a better flight. He put it on to save him from the jump to come. If anything, the hot coffee incident causes him to cling tighter to the parachute and even look forward to the jump.

If we have put on the Lord Jesus Christ for the right motive—to flee from the wrath to come—then when tribulation strikes, when the flight gets bumpy, we won't get angry at God, and we won't lose our joy and peace. Why should we? We didn't come to Christ for a better lifestyle, but to flee from the wrath to come.

If anything, tribulation drives the true believer *closer* to the Savior. Sadly, we have multitudes of professing Christians who lose their joy and peace when the flight gets bumpy. Why? They are the product of a man-centered gospel. They came lacking repentance, without which we cannot be saved.

What Was Pharaoh's Problem?

Why did it take so long for Pharaoh to bow to the will of the God of Israel? One would think that one plague would have caused him to immediately let God's people go. The answer is given to us in Exodus 9:27,28. After a number of terrible plagues, Pharaoh called for Moses and Aaron and said, "I have sinned this time. The Lord is righteous, and my people and I are wicked. Entreat the Lord, that there may be no more mighty thundering and hail, for it is enough. I will let you go, and you shall stay no longer." Such talk would seem to show that finally he was repentant. However, Exodus 9:30 gives insight as to what was still lacking. Moses said, "But as for you and your servants, I know that you will not yet fear the Lord God." Pharaoh saw his sin as something he had done "this time," and in his heart he didn't yet fear God enough to obey Him.

There are many who profess faith in the Savior who are like Pharaoh. A lack of knowledge of the Law has left them with a shallow understanding as to the exceedingly sinful nature of sin. They admit that they sinned "this time." They think sin is something they have done, rather than something that saturates their very nature. They lack the fear of God, and, like Pharaoh, these "believers" entreat the Lord simply because they find themselves in the midst of thunderous trials. Then, like the king of Egypt, when the plagues of life stop, they sin once again and harden their hearts to the will of God (Exodus 9:34).

What is it, then, that will break the will of a stubborn, rebellious sinner who gives mere lip service to God, but doesn't fear Him? The answer is, not only does he need to be terrified by the plagues of God's Law, but he also must see the death of the Firstborn. After the Law has done its terrifying work, the gospel will then give him light regarding the cost of his redemption. His heart will fear when he realizes that his liberty from wrath came through the death of the firstborn Son of God.

However, the death of Jesus of Nazareth, which purchased our salvation, didn't come swiftly. Jesus Himself told us that "Christ must suffer." When commenting on Psalm 22:14, Charles Spurgeon said:

> The placing of the cross in its socket had shaken Him with great violence, had strained all the ligaments, pained every nerve, and more or less dislocated all His bones. Burdened with His own weight, the august sufferer felt

the strain increasing every moment of those six long hours. His sense of faintness and general weakness were overpowering; while to His own consciousness He became nothing but a mass of misery and swooning sickness...To us, sensations such as our Lord endured would have been insupportable, and kind unconsciousness would have come to our rescue; but in His case, He was wounded, and felt the sword; He drained the cup and tasted every drop.

The risen Savior retained the scars of the cross for a reason. Calvary's grisly wounds must remain before the eyes of the Christian. They stand as a fearful testimony, not only of God's unfathomable love for sinners, but of His incredible love for justice.

In the next chapter, we are going to draw from the wisdom of men whose results the Church admires, but of whose methods many are sadly ignorant.

CHAPTER 11

Experience, the True Test

*L*et's now draw on the experiential wisdom of eminent men of God of the past. Martin Luther, in his commentary on Galatians, wrote: "Satan, the god of all dissension, stirreth up daily new sects, and last of all, which of all other I should never have foreseen or once suspected, he hath raised up a sect as such as teach...that men should not be terrified by the Law, but gently exhorted by the preaching of the grace of Christ." He was speaking of what he perceived as a satanic doctrine that was invading the Church of his day—a "sect" had risen which teaches that men should not be terrified by the Law, but gently exhorted by the preaching of the grace of Christ. His words perfectly describe the methods of most of contemporary evangelism. Modern evangelists would never think of using the Law to terrify, but instead, in ignorance they gently exhort by preaching the grace of Christ. Luther further stated, "The true function of the Law is to accuse and to kill; but the function of the gospel is to make alive."

J. C. Ryle wrote in *Holiness* of the sinner's motivation in coming to Christ:

> People will never set their faces decidedly towards heaven, and live like pilgrims, until they really feel that they are in danger of hell...Let us expound and beat out the Ten Commandments, and show the length, and

breadth, and depth, and height of their requirements.[5] This is the way of our Lord in the Sermon on the Mount. We cannot do better than follow His plan. We may depend on it, men will never come to Jesus, and stay with Jesus, and live for Jesus, unless they really know why they are to come, and what is their need. Those whom the Spirit draws to Jesus are those whom the Spirit has convinced of sin. Without thorough conviction of sin, men may seem to come to Jesus and follow Him for a season, but they will soon fall away and return to the world.

Isaac Watts, the great hymnwriter, said:

> I never knew but one person in the whole course of my ministry who acknowledged that the first motions of religion in his own heart arose from a sense of the goodness of God, "What shall I render to the Lord, who hath dealt so bountifully with me?" But I think all besides who have come within my notice have rather been first awakened to fly from the wrath to come by the passion of fear.

Dr. Martyn Lloyd-Jones spoke of the function of God's Law in gospel proclamation:

> The trouble with people who are not seeking for a Savior, and for salvation, is that they do not understand the nature of sin. It is the peculiar function of the Law to bring such an understanding to a man's mind and conscience. That is why great evangelical preachers 300 years ago in the time of the Puritans, and 200 years ago in the time of Whitefield and others, always engaged in what they called a preliminary "Law work."

John R. W. Stott, commenting on Galatians 3:23–29, said, "We cannot come to Christ to be justified until we have first been to Moses, to be condemned. But once we have gone to Moses, and acknowledged our sin, guilt and condemnation, we must not stay there. We must let Moses send us to Christ."

A Nazi soldier was once questioned about why he mercilessly shot Jewish women and children during World War II.
He told the interviewer that one of the motivations was
"curiosity." He calmly said, "I just fired and they fell." When
the interviewer asked if he felt bad about doing such things,
he said, "I was given 20 years, and I served 20 years." In
other words, he had paid his debt to society for his mis-
deeds. The scales were now balanced. Justice had been served.

However, when the interviewer asked him about his conscience, he refused to speak any further, and immediately
terminated the interview. Conscience speaks of more than
guilt for transgressions of *civil* law. The conscience bears witness to the Moral Law. It reminds men that there is a God
whose Law we have transgressed.

Paris Reidhead said these wonderfully wise words:

> If I had my way, I would declare a moratorium on
> public preaching of "the plan of salvation" in America for
> one to two years. Then I would call on everyone who has
> use of the airwaves and the pulpits to preach the holi-
> ness of God, the righteousness of God and the Law of
> God, until sinners would cry out, "What must we do to
> be saved?" Then I would take them off in a corner and
> whisper the gospel to them. Such drastic action is need-
> ed because we have gospel-hardened a generation of sin-
> ners by telling them how to be saved before they have
> any understanding why they need to be saved.
>
> Don't use John 3:16. Why? Because you tell a sinner
> how to be saved before he has realized that he needs to
> be saved. What you have done is gospel-hardened him.

What did he say? *"Don't use John 3:16."* That sounds like
heresy! However, I don't think D. L. Moody would consider
such advice unbiblical. Look at what he said:

> It is a great mistake to give a man who has not been
> convicted of sin certain passages that were never meant

for him. The Law is what he needs...Do not offer the consolation of the gospel until he sees and knows he is guilty before God. We must give enough of the Law to take away all self-righteousness. I pity the man who preaches only one side of the truth—always the gospel, and never the Law (*Pleasures and Profit of Bible Study*, Morgan and Scott Ltd., p. 111).

The Light Didn't Waken Him

Peter lay soundly asleep in Herod's prison (Acts 12:6). This is faith in action. Faith snoozes, even in a storm. Stephen had been stoned, James had just been killed with a sword—and Peter sleeps like a parishioner in the back row of a dead church. He was bound with chains between two soldiers. More guards stood before the door of the prison. Suddenly an angel of the Lord appeared and stood by him, "and a light shone in the cell." There is a strong inference that the light didn't awaken Peter from his sleep, because the Scriptures then tell us that the angel struck him on the side. As he arose, his chains fell off, he girded himself, tied on his shoes, put on his garment, and followed the angel. After that, the iron gate leading to the city opened of its own accord, and Peter was free.

The sinner is in the prison of his sins. He is taken captive by the devil. He is bound by the chains of sin, under the sentence of death. He is asleep in his sins. He lives in a dream world. But it isn't the gospel light that will awaken him. How can "Good News" alarm a sinner? No, the Law must strike him. He needs to be struck with the lightning of Sinai and awakened by its thunderings. That will rouse him to his plight of being on the threshold of death. Then he will arise and the gospel will remove the chains of sin and death. It will be "the power of God to salvation." Then he will gird himself with truth, tie on his gospel shoes, put on his garment of righteousness, follow the Lord, and the iron gate of the Celestial City will open of its own accord.

Our nation is full of people (both in and out of church) who have come under the light of the gospel, but who have never been struck by the Law. (In a later chapter, we will look at how many this may actually be.) They are still asleep in their sins, unaware of their terrible plight because the Law has never awakened them. The power of the Commandments must open their eyes before the light of the gospel can be of benefit. Look at this *sequence* in what Paul writes to the Ephesians: "Therefore He [the Lord] says, 'Awake you who sleep, arise from the dead, and Christ will give you light'" (Ephesians 5:14). There must be an awakening before Jesus Christ gives us light. Dr. Timothy Dwight, former president of Yale University, concluded: "Few, very few, are ever awakened or convinced by the encouragements and promises of the gospel, but almost all by the denunciations of the Law."

I received the following newsletter from someone in New York. This illustrates how the gospel makes little sense without the Law:

> We went to visit [our 96-year-old grandmother] every week and even though she has not received the gospel so freely these past few years, we kept sharing the truth of Jesus with her each time. Mike would play songs about Him. Wendy would talk to her. We would pray for her physical strength and add into the prayer how we wanted God to reveal His Son to Nana.
>
> Then last week, Wendy got the flu, and while she was in bed feeling miserable, she read Ray Comfort's book... which challenges us to share the whole gospel and not sugar-coat it. It talks about using the Law when talking to a sinner to make them see how they have personally broken God's Law and are doomed without a Savior who paid the price for them. It says in Psalm 19:7 that the "Law of the Lord is perfect, converting the soul." God spoke to Wendy's heart that she needed to share the Law

with Nana before Nana could ever see the grace and mercy of God in the cross.

So after committing the day and every detail to God, we went over to visit Nana. She was more alert and less distracted than usual. While Mike was praying, Wendy read her God's Commandments from Exodus 20:1–17 and then asked Nana pointblank, "Nana, have you ever lied? Or stolen anything, even a little thing?" She replied, "I guess so." Wendy shared about God's very real judgments, hell, and heaven, that one day Nana would be standing face to face before God and would have to give an account of her life. Then she read from Isaiah 53:5,6 and told Nana about Jesus and the horror of His cross. Nana looked shocked that someone would have those awful things happen to Him. Wendy shared some of her testimony and then asked Nana if she wanted to ask God to forgive her of her sins. She said *yes!* And she asked God to forgive her and wash her clean in the Blood of Jesus.

The 96-year-old didn't know that she was sinning against God until the Law in the hand of the Spirit did its work. Look at Martin Luther's comments on Romans 7:9 ("I was alive once without the Law, but when the commandment came, sin revived"):

So it is with the work-righteous and the proud unbelievers. Because they do not know the Law of God, which is directed against them, it is impossible for them to know their sin. Therefore also they are not amenable to instruction. If they would know the Law, they would also know their sin; and sin to which they are now dead would become alive in them.

Jonathan Edwards stated, "The only way we can know whether we are sinning is by knowing His Moral Law." George Whitefield said to his hearers, "First, then, before you can speak peace to your hearts, you must be made to see, made to feel, made to weep over, made to bewail, your actual transgressions against the Law of God." When we preach the whole counsel of God, we merely work with the Holy Spirit to convince men of sin. In *Today's Gospel: Authentic or Synthetic?*, Walter Chantry wrote:

> The absence of God's holy Law from modern preaching is perhaps as responsible as any other factor for the evangelistic impotence of our churches and missions. Only by the light of the Law can the vermin of sin in the heart be exposed. Satan has effectively used a very clever device to silence the Law, which is needed as an instrument to bring perishing men to Christ.
>
> It is imperative that preachers of today learn how to declare the spiritual Law of God; for, until we learn how to wound consciences, we shall have no wounds to bind with gospel bandages.

When we preach the whole counsel of God, we merely work with the Holy Spirit to convince men of sin.

Listen to John MacArthur saying the same thing: "God's grace cannot be faithfully preached to unbelievers until the Law is preached and man's corrupt nature is exposed. It is impossible for a person to fully realize his need for God's grace until he sees how terribly he has failed the standards of God's Law."

According to John Newton, "Ignorance of the nature and design of the Law is at the bottom of most religious mistakes." Charles Spurgeon stated, "I do not believe that any man can preach the gospel who does not preach the Law." Then he warns, "Lower the Law and you dim the light by which man perceives his guilt; this is a very serious loss to the sinner rather than a gain; for it lessens the likelihood of his conviction and conversion. I say you have deprived the gospel of its ablest auxiliary [its most powerful weapon] when you have set aside the Law. You have taken away from it the schoolmaster that is to bring men to Christ... *They will never accept grace till they tremble before a just and holy Law.* Therefore the Law serves a most necessary purpose, and it must not be removed from its place."

Look at how the Law did its part in bringing Robert Flockhart, one of Spurgeon's favorite preachers, to the cross:

> I consider the language of the apostle in Romans 7:9 not inapplicable to my situation at that time, "but when the commandment came, sin revived, and I died." Sin, that had been asleep before, came like a giant upon me. I saw myself in the mirror of God's Law. That Law was spiritual and extended to the thoughts and intents of my heart. Dreadful and blasphemous thoughts, like sparks out of a chimney, now came out of my heart. I was afraid to open my Bible or even to look up, for fear the Lord would send a thunderbolt out of heaven to crush me.
>
> What a translation from darkness to light, from the kingdom of darkness to the kingdom of God's dear Son! My guilt removed and my pardon sealed, peace flowed like a river into my soul (*The Street Preacher*, pp. 77,81).

Perhaps modern evangelism's reticence to preach what produces fear is simply due to concern about the reaction of sinners. Some may worry that the message may be aligned with what is commonly called "hell-fire" preaching. Yet there is a vast difference between the use of the Law and hell-fire preaching. Understandably, the thought of the existence of hell, without the use of the Law to justify its existence, is unreasonable to a sinner's mind. How could a God of love create a place of eternal torment? Imagine if the police suddenly burst into your home, thrust you into prison, and angrily shouted, "You are going away for a long time!" Such conduct would undoubtedly leave you bewildered and angry. What they have done is *unreasonable*.

However, if the law burst into your home and instead told you specifically why you were in trouble by saying, "We have discovered 10,000 marijuana plants growing in your backyard. You are going away for a long time!" at least you would understand why you are in trouble. Knowledge of the law you transgressed furnished you with understanding. It makes judgment *reasonable*.

Hell-fire preaching without use of the Law to show the sinner why God is angry with him will more than likely leave him bewildered and angry—for what he considers unreasonable punishment. However, when we use the Law lawfully, it appeals to the "reason" of sinners. Paul *reasoned* with Felix about judgment to come and his sins, to the point where the governor "was afraid" (Acts 24:25). Hell became reasonable. No doubt the "righteousness" Paul spoke of was the righteousness which is of the Law, and the result was that the fear of God fell upon the heart of his hearer.

Those who come to the Savior with such knowledge are not strangers to fear, even after the cross. They tremble at the cost of their redemption. They gaze with fear-filled hearts at the grizzly sight of Calvary's cross. They work out their own salvation with "fear and trembling" because they were not redeemed "with silver and gold, but with the precious Blood of Christ."

In his wonderful book *Fresh Wind, Fresh Fire*, Jim Cymbala, rightly frustrated by the lukewarm contemporary Church, says of the disciples:

> Once they were empowered on the Day of Pentecost, however, they became the church victorious, the church militant. With the gracious manifestation of God's Spirit in the Upper Room, the disciples encountered their first audience. Peter, the biggest failure of them all, became

the preacher that day. It was no homiletical masterpiece, to be sure. But people were deeply convicted—"cut to the heart," according to Acts 2:37—by his anointed words. Three thousand were gathered into the church that day (p. 92).

The inference is that the key was the empowerment of the Holy Spirit. This is true. However, we have the same Holy Spirit nowadays, and we rarely see such a harvest of souls. Why not? Simply because Peter properly prepared the ground upon which he was sowing. His audience was composed of "devout men" who were gathered at Pentecost to celebrate the giving of God's Law on Mount Sinai.

Even though these were godly Jews, Peter told them that they were "lawless"—that they had violated God's Law by murdering Jesus (Acts 2:23). He drove home that fact by saying, "Therefore let all the house of Israel know assuredly that God has made this Jesus, *whom you crucified*, both Lord and Christ" (Acts 2:36, italics added). It was then that they saw that their sin was personal. They were "cut to the heart" and cried out for help. Only after the Law convicted them of their sinfulness did Peter offer them grace (v. 38).

This was also the case with Nicodemus and Nathanael. Nicodemus was a leader of the Jews whom Jesus called a "teacher of Israel" (John 3:10). He was therefore thoroughly versed in God's Law. He also had a humble heart. Here was a leader of the Jews acknowledging the deity of the Son of God (John 3:2). The Law was a schoolmaster to bring this humble, godly Jew to Christ.

According to John 1:47, Jesus said that Nathanael was an Israelite (brought up under the Law) in whom there was "no deceit" (he didn't twist the Law as the Pharisees did; he no doubt read "the way of God in truth"). The Law also served as a schoolmaster to bring this godly Jew to the Savior.

CHAPTER 12

The Badge of Authority

*A*merica has chosen to live in moral darkness. Its Constitution has replaced Holy Scripture as the point of moral reference. The writings of men have become sacred. Contemporary America is no different than the Pharisees of Christ's time, whose decrees made the Word of God void.

Take, for instance, pornography. Why should our government tolerate such moral perversion? To them, the answer is clear from the writings of our forefathers—it is a "constitutional right" to produce unclean literature, even if it is morally offensive. However, ask a man who advocates pornographic literature if *child* porn is legitimate, and he will usually draw his moral line. Ask him then at what age "immoral" child porn crosses the divide and becomes "morally acceptable." You will find, with a little digging, that the dividing line is the line of *personal pleasure*. He doesn't gain pleasure from a 13-year-old child, but does from a 17-year-old young woman. His love for sin clouds his moral judgment.

The Constitution of the United States is being used for something it was never intended. When a legal document is employed as a moral beacon, we end up with morally blind legislators leading a morally blind nation. Both fall into a dirty ditch. However, the argument for pornography is concluded with one statement from Holy Scripture: "Whoever looks at a woman to lust for her has already committed adultery with her in his heart" (Matthew 5:28). Case closed.

When we specifically point to the Scriptures as an ethical beacon, we must make it clear to those who will listen that our express reference is the Moral Law of God. There is great reason for this. In 1989, when I first came to the United States, I was preaching in the open air at Venice Beach, California. Unbeknown to me at that time, the police there wore shorts and rode around on bicycles.

When I stood on a soapbox and began to speak on the edge of the wide sidewalk, a crowd of about 80 people gathered around to listen. Suddenly, a man in shorts stood right in front of me and told me to stop. When I ignored him, he became very indignant and told me once again to stop. I asked, "Are you a police officer?" He then became angry and said through gritted teeth, "If you don't stop right now, I will arrest you!"

It was then that I noticed a badge on his belt, which told me he *was* an officer of the law. Suddenly, his words carried a great deal of authority! I was elevated above him, and his badge was out of my sight, so I had no respect for him other than what I would give an ordinary civilian.

Those who are representatives of the living God, yet who don't point to the Law as the core of their authority, will not gain due consideration from the world. Jesus stood before the multitudes as One who was a representative of the Law of God. The Bible says the Messiah would bring justice to the earth and that the "coastlands will wait for His law" (Isaiah 42:4). He repeatedly referred to the Law as the point of His authority, saying, "I did not come to destroy [the Law] but to fulfill," "One jot or one tittle will by no means pass from the Law," "This is the Law and the Prophets," "Have you not read in the Law...?" "It is easier for heaven and earth to pass away than for one tittle of the law to fail" (Matthew 5:17,18; 7:12;

Luke 16:17).

Abortion is wrong. Adultery is wrong. Pornography is wrong. We can shout our moral convictions from the highest housetops, but the world will not listen. It exalts itself above the claims of the Christian faith. It has no incentive to open its heart to what we have to say.

Why did I suddenly take notice of the man who was telling me to stop? *It was his badge that caused me to take notice.* His badge said that if I didn't heed his words there would be coming judgment. To tell the world that it's wrong to kill, to steal, to commit adultery, without reference to future punishment, is to point an unloaded cannon.

Some may listen because morality does have positive influences. Theft can ravage a society. Adultery can ruin families. Lying can shatter friendships. In that context morality makes sense. However, when we tell the world to repent because God has "appointed a day on which He will judge the world in righteousness" (Acts 17:31), they will have an inducement to obey the gospel. It will begin to dawn on them that their own eternal welfare is at stake.

Again, for the Church to neglect to point to the Law of God is to hide the badge of our authority from the world. Understandably, sinners will disregard what we have to say. The gospel we preach is only there because God stands by the holiness of the Law. If eternal Law didn't exist, then there would have been no need for a sacrifice. The Law demands retribution. It was the divine fire of God's Law that fell on the sacrifice of Calvary.

If the world *knew* that there is an Eternal Law they must face, that the Law necessitates death and hell for transgression, then they would seriously consider the claims of the gospel. If they understood that the long arm of the Law will reach right down into the heart of humanity, they would repent. If they knew that Almighty God is angry at the wicked every day, that His wrath abides on them, they would flee to the Savior.

Let me put it another way. Each of the Ten Commandments is of itself a "key." However, these are not keys that *release*; instead, they are keys that lock the sinner in the holding cell of sin and death. Paul spoke of being "kept under guard" by the Law. He was left without hope, condemned, waiting for capital punishment from the hand of the Law he had so blatantly violated.

When speaking of God's Law, Charles Spurgeon said, "Having thus removed the mask and shown the desperate case of the sinner, the relentless Law causes the offense to abound yet more by bringing home the sentence of condemnation. It mounts the judgment seat, puts on the black cap and pronounces the sentence of death. With a harsh unpitying voice it solemnly thunders forth the words 'condemned already!'"

It was in the darkness of the Law that Paul saw the light of the glorious gospel.

It was in the darkness of the Law that Paul saw the light of the glorious gospel. The grace of God pointed him to another door—the Door of the Savior. He could leave the cell because his fine had been paid in full by the shed blood of the spotless Lamb of God. It was the Law that showed Paul that he was unable to save himself. He knew that salvation was an act of mercy—that his deliverance from death was the result of God's grace, not something in his own character that drew mercy toward him.

This principle was clearly illustrated recently when I had been preaching open-air in the Third Street Promenade of Santa Monica, California, where I have a permit to speak. I had been taking a team there each Friday night for more than two years, and only once before had I seen such antagonism toward the gospel. There was the usual bitter animosity from the products of modern evangelism. One man, betraying his "Christian" background, started preaching about his hamster dying for the sins of the world, and if only we would give our hearts to him, we would find peace and joy. When a professing atheist named James began to mock the things of God by yelling "Praise Jesus" among other things, my suspicions were confirmed when he confided that he had once given his heart to Christ. A sweet teenage girl, a Mormon, kept shouting that I was Satan, and tried to shock me by baring her breasts (I looked the other way). Others were spitting and using language that would make your hair curl tighter than a pig's tail. Among a number of others, three teenage girls came to the "heckler's" microphone and said that they were witches. A few years ago I would have doubted what they said, but I believed their testimony.

We have a mannequin (a dummy) called Lazarus, who quietly lies under a sheet as a crowd-getter. People often stop and ask, "What have you got *that* there for?" To which I say, "It's to get people to stop and ask, 'What have you got *that* there for?' It works, doesn't it?"

On this particular night, Lazarus received his share of persecution. One young man began doing lewd acts on him, much to the delight of the crowd. While I was speaking, another youth burst into the crowd, rushed up to Lazarus, and stomped on his head. It was such a violent act that Lazarus' plastic face actually burst. I jumped off my soapbox, grabbed the youth by his shirt, and said, "That dummy cost me a lot of money. Give me $80 right now or you are in big trouble." I looked him in the eyes and said, "You are under citizen's arrest for willful damage of my property. I'm calling the police."

He looked scared and said, "You can have everything I

have." He immediately handed me a fistful of dollars. I passed it to a friend, who counted it and said that there was only $28. I told the youth that wasn't enough and I wanted the full $80. He protested that he didn't have any more cash.

By this time a large crowd had gathered, so (still holding the youth by the shirt) I said, "Just as I am holding this man because he has transgressed the law, so God has placed you in a holding cell for transgression of *His* Law. The sentence for your crimes against God is death."

I then went through the Law into grace and said, "God is rich in mercy and sent His Son to pay the fine for you." I preached the cross, faith, and repentance...still holding the young man tightly by his shirt. I told the crowd that because Jesus paid the fine in full for us on the cross, God can extend His mercy toward us. We are free to go.

Then I turned to the youth, stuffed the money in his hand, and said, "Here's your money back. Neither am I going to call the police. You are free to go."

It was such a clear illustration of God's mercy. The young man's guilt was evident (he had been caught in the act). He couldn't make atonement. He *deserved* nothing but judgment, but instead received mercy. His mouth dropped open in unbelief.

Sin's Pleasure

Someone once called me and asked for my advice about a publication he wanted to produce. It was to help men who were addicted to pornography. He was going to write his experience in tract form, relating how pornography had ruined him. The vice produced guilt, ruined his marriage, and made him a slave to his passions. His thought was that the negative fruit of the sin would steer men away from it. His philosophy sounds good, but it rarely works. If it did, we wouldn't have so many people smoking cigarettes, abusing drugs, gambling, and drinking alcohol. The evidence that smoking results in a slow and painful death doesn't deter smokers. Drug abuse kills. Gambling destroys homes and lives. Cities with legalized gambling have been found to have higher rates of crime, suicide, bankruptcy, and other social ills; yet, people gamble. Multitudes still blindly dive into a sea of poison called alcohol, despite the mass of dead bodies piled on the shore.

People know the consequences of a sinful lifestyle, but the immediate pleasure *far* outweighs the fear of long-term negative consequences. Sinful man will not give up his darling lust unless he has a good reason to. Hell is a good reason.

In the next chapter, we'll look at how the Ten Commandments can be used effectively in personal witnessing.

CHAPTER 13

Don't Leave Me Like This!

I was in Baltimore without a meeting on a Sunday night, so I decided to change my plane ticket to go home early. When I called, the reservation agent gave the name of the airline, told me her name was Fran, and asked how she could be of help to me. I explained my situation, and made her laugh a little to a point where I had the liberty to ask about her spiritual life. I said, "Fran, are you a Christian?" She answered, "No. I don't accept the virgin birth." I explained to her that wasn't the issue with her at the moment, and that her big problem was the Ten Commandments. I asked, "Have you ever told a lie?" She said she had. She also admitted that she had stolen. When I explained that Jesus said that lust was the same as adultery in God's sight, and asked her if she had lusted, she said, "Of course."

I said, "Fran, by your own admission, you are a lying, thieving, adulterer-at-heart. You have to face God on Judgment Day, *and we have looked at only three of the Ten Commandments.*" I then said, "I would like a window seat if possible." She didn't appreciate the subject change, and said, *"Don't leave me like this!"* Gently, I said, "What's wrong Fran, don't you like being left with your conscience?" I further went on to reason with her about her salvation, about Judgment Day, then the cross.

We shouldn't be afraid to make the sinner tremble. Which is worse: a little trembling because of guilt, or eternity in the lake of fire? Men like Whitefield and others preached until the Law "stopped the mouth" and sinners hung their heads in shame. They weren't afraid to use the terrors of the Law to drive men to the cross. A resurrected and accusing conscience is the first evidence of the beginnings of the work of the Holy Spirit. It is a great mistake to muffle its voice with talk of God's forgiveness before it has a chance to do its precious work.

A resurrected and accusing conscience is the first evidence of the beginnings of the work of the Holy Spirit.

Fran didn't get mad at me. I wasn't judging her. *She* was the one who admitted her sins. Besides, what could she say: "I thought lying, theft, etc., were right"? She couldn't *begin* to justify her sins in light of her quickened conscience. It is because of the ally of the "work of the Law" that we can gently say "hard" things to sinners.

It is interesting to note that the conscience doesn't join in with the pleasures of sin. The unregenerate person loves sin with all of his heart, mind, soul, and strength. However, the judge in the courtroom of the mind stands aloof and makes an impartial judgment. It is the "conscience also bearing witness,...their thoughts accusing or else excusing them" (Romans 2:15). The judge gives a *guilty* or *not guilty* verdict of what is evidenced before it.

In parts of Africa during the drought season, antelope are drawn by thirst to pools of muddy water. Without drink they will die of dehydration. Hidden in the foul waters lie hungry and vicious crocodiles. The only thing visible in the water, to the discerning, is the naked eye of the monster as it watches the antelope's every movement.

Desire so consumes the animal that he slowly ventures to

the water's edge, and completely lets down his God-given guard as he drinks in the life-giving liquid. Instinct warns him of the danger, but his unquenchable thirst drives him to the water. Suddenly, great jaws open and amid the splashing of water, the animal is pulled to a terrifying death.

The sinner is drawn to the muddy pool of iniquity by his uncontrollable thirst for sin. The cries of his God-given conscience are muffled at the sight of what lies before him. Suddenly, death seizes upon him in an instant and he is gone forever, swallowed by the jaws of everlasting hell.

The Law reveals the crocodile *before* it attacks. As the sinner drinks in the waters of sin, he suddenly sees sin's terrible form as it lies hidden in the pool. This is what Paul is speaking about in Romans 7:8–12. The Law showed him the appetite in the eye of the beast, causing him to quickly draw back from the pool of iniquity.

So Long, Pal!

We regularly receive calls on our 800 number from dyslexic people who misdial the number they are calling. Very early one morning a deep-voiced gentleman phoned, thinking he was calling a company that sells farm supplies. I told him that he had transposed the last two digits, then said to make sure he read his Bible. He said he wouldn't, because he was an atheist. For the next few minutes I reasoned with him about the necessity of having a maker for everything that was made. It was a spirited fight, but it was merely swordplay. The moment would come when I would have to get my point across, to go for the kill. I took the Commandments in hand and lunged toward the heart: "Do you think you have kept the Ten Commandments?" He said he thought he had. "Have you ever told a lie?" He had, but would not hold still for a second and admit that he was a liar. He jumped back and forth, insisting that someone who told lies was "human," or told "fibs" or was "weak, like everyone else."

When I pressed the point, he suddenly spat out, "Okay, I'm a liar!" We touched on two other Commandments which he admitted to transgressing, the existence of his conscience, and the fact of Judgment Day. Suddenly, his references to evolution, other people's sins, and hypocrisy in the Church were no longer the issue. He was mortally wounded...cut to the heart. He staggered backward and protested, *"I'm a good person!"* I thrust back, "No, you're not. You're a lying thief!" The pain was too much for him. He said, *"So long, pal!"* and hung up in my ear.

I sat by the phone and wished that he had stayed in the fight for another minute. I would have told him that he was just adding self-righteousness to his sin. I would also have liked to tell him to study Matthew 24 and Luke 21, which would prove to him that the Bible is the Word of the Creator. Then I prayed that God's hand would be on him.

About ten seconds later, the phone rang again. When I picked it up, I heard a deep-voiced and mystified man mumble, "What's going on? How did I get you again? I tried to call this number, and instead I get one that makes my blood hot!"

Hot blood means that life is present. He was no longer a cold-blooded atheist. *I was beside myself with joy.* I told him to read Matthew 24 and Luke 21. Then I gave him my name and said he could call our 800 number anytime. When he kept mumbling, "Why did I call you again?" I could think of only two alternatives. Either he was a dummy and had called the wrong number again, or God's hand was upon him. I told him that it was because God's hand was upon him. He didn't argue about that, and this time our parting was more congenial.

Right Number

It was a Friday afternoon. The phone rang, and when I answered it I heard, "Is this Direct Imports?" I said it wasn't and asked what number the man wanted. He gave our number so I said, "Well, that is our number, but before you go, *make sure you read your Bible.*" He became quiet, then asked, "Why's that?" I said so that he could find how to secure his eternal destiny and added, "And there's nothing more important than that, is there?" He said, "Yi, yi, yi...*I'd better sit down for this!*" I asked, "Are you Jewish?" When he said he was, I told him that I was also Jewish and remarked, "Remember, you've got to face the Ten Commandments on Judgment Day."

His reply was interesting: "I have done research, specifically on the adultery one, and I've come to the conclusion that you can fool around with a woman, as long as she's not married." I said, "If you as much as look with lust, the Bible says that you commit adultery in your heart. Have you ever told a lie?" He had. I asked if he had stolen; he had. So I gently told him that he was, by his own admission, a lying, thieving adulterer, and that's why he needed the Savior Jesus Christ— to save him from God's anger. I told him to read his Bible and seek God for the salvation of his soul. I also invited him to call my number anytime if he wanted to talk in the future. His voice sounded quite depressed as he said, "Thank you very much for talking to me." I think I ruined his weekend.

In the following chapter we're going to look closely at a very important question: What is it that sparks a burning flame of passion for the lost in the heart of a believer?

CHAPTER 14

Take Two Tablets and Call Me When You're Mourning

Why are there so few front-line soldiers within the Body of Christ? There are many who say that they love God, read the Word, pray, and praise God with a passion, but there are so few who have what Spurgeon referred to as a deep "tenderness." These are the ones who carry an anguish of soul for the fate of the ungodly. They break out of their complacency and seek by any means to save that which is lost. The love of Christ "compels" them (2 Corinthians 5:14). The Greek word used denotes that His love arrests them, preoccupies and presses them to reach out to the lost. These are the ones of whom Jesus said there was a great and tragic lack (Matthew 9:37,38), commanding us to pray that God would give us more. They take off their jackets of condescension, put on the armor of light, and go to battle.

For years I couldn't discover what it was that forged these rare and hardy souls. Were these merely diamonds that sparkled more than others because of a God-given temperament? Were these people born fearless by nature and their bold and zealous witness came naturally to them, outsparkling others who lacked such a virtue? No, some of the most zealous and bold witnesses of Christ I have known have been of a quiet or even a shy disposition.

One night in late 1994, I found the answer. A friend,

Pastor Mike Smalley, and I were at the home of Winkie and Faye Pratney deep in the heart of Texas. Winkie is a fellow New Zealander, so it was something special for us to get together for dinner—it called for steak.

Winkie went outside to put the steaks on a barbecue, but a few minutes later reluctantly brought them back inside when the barbie ran out of propane gas. As he cooked them inside, he said something about them not being as tender as they would have been if he had cooked them on the intense heat of the barbecue.

After a few minutes, the entire house filled with smoke from his cooking; but it was well worth it—the steaks melted in the mouth. Besides, the fans in the house soon cleared the air.

When I remarked about the tenderness of my steak, Winkie shared his secret. He explained that the way to keep a steak tender is to sear it on both sides for forty seconds on a very hot hotplate. That seals the juices in the steak, then you cook it slowly until it is done.

About 3:00 a.m. the following morning, it dawned on me about what produces the much-desired tenderhearted Christian. When a sinner comes under the intense heat of the Law of God, it has the effect of sealing within him a tender heart. This is how it happens: As the spirituality of the Law bears down on him, it shows him the exceeding sinfulness of his heart. It reveals to him that the very core of his nature is vile, that his lust is adultery, that hatred is murder, that he is a liar, a thief, and a rebel—a selfish and ungrateful sinner.

He begins to see that he has loved what is abhorrent to his Creator. The Law shows him that even his so-called "good" works are tainted by a self-centered motive. This knowledge coupled with the fact that he has *greatly* angered God by transgressing His Law, and that hell is his just dessert, is the "heat" that seals in the tenderness of soul.

When grace is revealed, it is embraced as a man dying of thirst embraces a jug of water. The experience of the searing heat of the Law bringing him to the point of death, yet being freely given the waters of life, forever secures the virtue of unspeakable gratitude. And that makes him a laborer for life. The Law gives him understanding that in the gospel he is forgiven much, so he loves much—vertically and therefore horizontally.

Such tenderness is difficult to cultivate in someone who already possesses knowledge of God's grace in Christ. His realization of God's goodness deprives him of the fear of wrath. Only those who can sing "and grace my fears relieved" see grace as being truly amazing. This is why I believe it is a mistake to tell a guilty unregenerate sinner "God loves you." Such knowledge doesn't allow fear to enter his heart. That deprives him of a depth of gratitude he would otherwise have if fear had been allowed to do its work.

Only those who can sing "and grace my fears relieved" see grace as being truly amazing.

This is why the enlightened witness of Christ is not afraid to gently put on the heat when speaking with sinners. He knows that when the smoke of the wrath of the Law condemns the prisoner before him, it is actually preparing his heart for a pardon that will be welcomed *because of the fear gripping the prisoner's heart.* The Christian knows that the tears that fear produces will be wiped away by the gentle hand of God's grace. He knows that that hand will not be fully appreciated if the Law is not allowed to do its most necessary work. It is the Law of God that exposes sin, and when sin is viewed under the penetrating light of the Law, as we have seen, it makes grace "abound." The Greek word used to explain this in Romans 5:20 is *hyperperisseuo,* which means to "superabound."

If I were a physician and I knew you had a terrible disease, I would be unwise to give you a cure without first carefully explaining to you that you had the disease. However, I wouldn't merely tell you that you had the disease; I would actually let fear work for your good. I would use it to cause you to *want* to take the cure. As I showed you x-rays, I would watch beads of sweat drip from your brow and say to myself, "Good, he's beginning to see the seriousness of his disease." The fear will not only cause you to embrace the cure, it will (when the cure is received) give you tremendous appreciation for me as your doctor for providing the cure.

A great preacher once asked a well-known actor how it was that when performers present a story they often bring the audience to tears, yet rarely do ministers move a congregation to such a degree. The actor responded that they portray fiction as if it were a reality, while ministers of the gospel too often portray reality as if it were fiction.

If we really believed souls were going to hell, we would preach with overwhelming passion. Our hearts would groan in constant prayer. We would run to sinners with solemn words of warning, take hold of them and beseech them to turn from sin. Instead, we lack any real sense of urgency. We are afraid to speak frankly with sinners about their personal sins. We think that searing them under the heat of the Law will do harm rather than good. But consider how Jesus spoke with the woman at the well in John chapter 4. He applied the heat of the Law to her (v. 18) and spoke of her *personal* transgressions—and what was the result? She became an immediate laborer (vv. 28,29).[6]

I received the following letter about one of my books, which shows the power of the Law to bring a thirst for righteousness:

> This friend of mine has always told me for the last

eight years whenever the opportunity popped up, that the Law was finished with and that the Ten Commandments were basically useless. Of course, I tried to gently suggest that the knowledge of sin could not come by any other way than the Law, but this was always smothered in a sugary reference to love and grace...so I kept quiet.

But I stuck my neck out last week and gave the book to this friend, and the next day he handed it back to me. He was crying and shaking with emotion. He could hardly speak. He said, "I've just been born again!" What really happened, I think, was the full impact of the power of God's Law had struck him and wounded him, showing him clearly how bad his sin really was. He was in quite a state for several days after that, and kept breaking out into praise to God.

It was the two tablets of the Law that caused the mourning in his heart.

Seven Scared Sinners

Late in 1994, I arrived in Baton Rouge to do a series of meetings. A young man named Jeff picked me up and told me of the plan he had for me to speak open-air at a fake funeral.

After a short sleep in my hotel I was picked up, briefed the pallbearers, the corpse, and the crowd as to the do's and don'ts of an open-air setting, then we drove to the site of the preaching.

When we pulled into the parking lot of a Wal-Mart I thought we were going to buy something, but it was actually the location Jeff had chosen for us. After about five minutes of preaching, one of the security guards approached me and said I could speak for another five minutes, then I had to stop. I was thankful for the extra time, and afterwards mentioned this to the local pastor who had come with us. He smiled and said, "When you started, I told the security guard, 'See all those people around the preacher? They go to my church and we all shop at Wal-Mart.'"

After that, we drove to an area near the local university campus and set up the funeral once again. This time Jeff had decided he would give my voice a break by preaching himself. Just as we were organizing the pallbearers, a siren shrieked behind me. I turned to see a traffic officer on a motorcycle angrily waving over a van full of teenagers. As the van pulled to the side of the road the police officer jumped off his bike, ran to the van, opened the door, and cursed the driver. He then grabbed him, violently pulled him out of his seat, and thrust him against the vehicle. The officer then gave him a body search, once again using obscenities as he did so. The scared youth didn't resist as he was frisked and yelled at.

From what I could gather, the officer had waved the van over and they had failed to stop. Some of the passengers in the van had thought the incident funny, which had caused the officer to boil over. Here was a wrath-filled, slightly out-of-control officer of the law, "God's minister, an avenger to execute wrath on him who practices evil" (Romans 13:4).

We decided that it wouldn't be wise to preach with the law so upset, so we moved to the entrance of a bar about 30 yards across the parking lot. While Jeff preached, semi-drunken teenagers came out of the bar and mocked him. It was a replay of what I had just seen in the natural realm. These teens were refusing to listen to the Law, and they were storing up wrath that would be revealed on the Day of Wrath. The Day would come when an angry Law would pull them from the seat of the scornful, and from that there will be no escape.

After about five minutes, the manager came out and stopped Jeff from preaching (the local church members didn't patronize his bar).

As we wandered back to the van, we passed the youths

the officer had stopped. I went over to the group and asked what had happened. The driver was obviously still upset and told me that he had driven through a stop sign, had his lights out, and had failed to stop when the officer first waved him over. His six friends who were with him were also shaken by what had taken place. I couldn't help but sympathize a little with the driver and shared how I thought the officer had clearly lost control of himself. He agreed.

I wanted to witness to them, but felt I lacked the right approach. They were like a distressed child who had just grazed his leg, and I had arrived to put salt in the wound. I was sure that if I mentioned sin, righteousness, and judgment at that point I would be told in no uncertain and colorful terms to depart from the area. I reluctantly told them I would see them later and walked back to our group.

As I stood there, someone asked if I had witnessed to them. I said I hadn't. I told the person that I didn't know how to approach the subject and that I needed a little time to get some thoughts together.

A moment later, I walked back to them determined to say something about their eternal salvation, even if I did get abused. Suddenly, I remembered that I had put about ten one-dollar bills in my wallet to give away at the open-air, something I often do to illustrate a number of points. When I asked how much the fine would be, the driver looked up and said, "About $200." I took my wallet out, pulled out the handful of bills and said, "This isn't much, but I would like to give this toward the fine." As I referred to the money, I looked down at it in amazement. Clearly visible in the middle of the wad of bills was a $10 bill, making it look like far more than it was. *It looked like a fortune!*

Different teens in the group said, "Wow...you can't do that...that's really nice of you...you don't even know us." The driver graciously declined the money, but the offer struck a chord in their hearts. They could see that I really cared for them and the suggestion had given me license to speak to them about their salvation. I said, "I'm a preacher. Here is a gift for each of you." I then handed each of them a penny with the Ten Commandments pressed onto it, and asked if they had kept the Law. When I asked if they had lied, stolen, lusted, etc., every one of them admitted they had broken the Commandments.

Then I turned to the driver and asked him if he was scared when the law pulled him from his vehicle. He said he was terrified. I then said, "Tonight you transgressed civil law, but now you know that you have also transgressed the Divine Law. If civil law scared you, wait until you face God on Judgment Day...it is a fearful thing to fall into the hands of the living God." I explained the gospel, asked if they had Bibles, and told them to dust them off and read the Gospel of John. I then shook their hands and thanked them for listening to me, and left them in the hands of a faithful Creator.

"Now you know that you have transgressed the Divine Law. If civil law scared you, wait until you face God on Judgment Day."

While I had been speaking, the driver was peeling masking tape from around his ankles. He had strapped sealed plastic bags of whiskey under his socks —something the law hadn't found when he was frisked. God only knows what may have happened that night if the driver had downed the whiskey and driven home with six drunken friends in his van.

The officer of the law missed that hidden offense, but God's Law won't miss a thing.

Both the civil and the Divine Law did a deep work in some young hearts that night. It was my prayer that seven "steaks" were seared to a crisp, and that some day seven tenderhearted and faithful laborers would enter the harvest fields and gladly toil for their Master.

By the way, Winkie Pratney's talents were not confined to cooking steak. The man is not only an excellent Bible teacher and author, but a brilliant ping-pong player as well, as I found out two days later. I also discovered that his style of demonstrative play was reminiscent of a pregnant woman in the latter stages of labor. Despite the sweat, groans, and screams when the man missed a shot, I learned that he was extremely talented. He played with the grace of a master. His speed, his genius, his reflexes, his dazzling shots were executed with astounding agility. Only occasionally does one get to witness such incredible brilliance.

I beat him.

CHAPTER 15

An Angry God

*I*f our theology leaves out the Law and thus the necessity of the Holy Spirit's conviction of sin, we will see nothing wrong with leaving a sinner with false peace. Remember that in Jeremiah 8:11 God said of the prophets and priests of Israel:

> They have healed the hurt of the daughter of My people slightly, saying, "Peace, peace!" when there is no peace.

This is how to give false peace to a sinner. Simply ask, "Do you have assurance that you will go to heaven when you die?" Who in his right mind doesn't want to go to heaven? So a good number will say something like, "I *hope* I'm going to heaven when I die." Now say, "God wants you to have that assurance. All of us have sinned and come short of the glory of God, but God sent His Son to die on the cross for us so that we could have peace with God. When we repent and trust in Him, God will give us everlasting life. He writes our name in the Book of Life. Would you like to accept Jesus into your heart right now and have your name written in heaven? I could lead you in what's called a 'sinner's prayer' right now. Would you like to pray?" Many do.

You may ask a predictable, "What's wrong with that?" Let me see if I can answer that question with an anecdote:

A blind sinner is unwittingly heading for a thousand-foot cliff. Modern evangelism draws alongside him and says,

"Blind man, I am going to give you a wonderful gift that will give you peace." He then takes a CD player and adjusts its earphones over his ears. The sightless man hears "Amazing Grace" being sung by a choir of ten thousand voices. His blind eyes widen with delight. He smiles and says, "What you said is true. This is truly wonderful. Thank you very much." He shakes the man's hand, turns up the volume on his newfound gift, and continues tapping his way toward the thousand-foot cliff.

What has modern evangelism done? It has failed to awaken the blind sinner to his true plight. Instead, it has given him *false* peace. Now he is not only still heading toward a horrible death, *but he is deaf toward any further verbal warning.* It has done an unspeakable disservice to the blind sinner.

Millions have been given assurance of salvation, but are strangers to biblical repentance. The Law has never awakened them. They have never been warned to turn from the cliffs of eternal destruction. Now, because of the techniques of contemporary evangelism, their ears are deaf to the true message of salvation.

A religious studies professor named Wade Clark Roof, in his book *Spiritual Marketplace: Baby Boomers and the Remaking of American Religion,* says that one-third of America's seventy-seven million Baby Boomers identify themselves as "born-again Christians." According to Roof, that means they've had a "highly personal spiritual experience that has changed their lives." Roof says only about half of those who call themselves "born again" today attend a conservative Protestant church. Twenty percent don't belong to *any* church at all, and a third of those who say they're "born again" believe in astrology and reincarnation.

There is even another hidden tragedy that has resulted from the efforts of modern evangelism. It doesn't take a rocket scientist to see that this nation has lost God's blessing. The American Cancer Society estimated that in just one year there were 1,382,400 new cancer cases. Add to that an onslaught of killer bees, massive hurricanes, devastating floods, earthquakes, droughts, tornadoes, etc. After years of evangelization by modern preachers, most of America's concept of God is one of a *benevolent* Father figure. Therefore, the terrible tragedies of "natural" disasters and deadly diseases that come her way are considered the mere rumblings of Mother Nature, El Niño, La Niña, global warming, global cooling—anything *but* the dealings of a holy God with a sinful nation. The thought that a God who is love would judge our nation with these catastrophes is unthinkable to many.

From there comes a tragic dilemma in which the Church finds herself: To go from preaching "God loves you" to "God is angry at the wicked every day" is too great a leap for her to take. Consequently, few preachers have the courage to say that America is under God's judgment, and those who do so are considered a little fanatical. Again, this is simply because just over one hundred years ago, modern evangelism forsook the scriptural *stepping stone*: the Law of God. Without it, the world cannot conceive that God would be angry at humanity. Remember, without the use of the Law, judgment is totally *unreasonable*. C. S. Lewis said, "When we merely say that we are bad, the 'wrath' of God seems a barbarous doctrine; as soon as we perceive our badness, it appears inevitable, a mere corollary from God's goodness." The Law helps us perceive our badness.

God is Nice

A sincere young lady once heckled me as I expounded the Ten Commandments to a crowd of mainly unsaved people. She boldly called out, "Don't listen to this man! *God loves you.*" I stopped speaking and asked her if she cared about the salvation of those to whom I was speaking. She said she did, so I gently coaxed her up onto the soapbox and asked her to give her testimony. After she had (bravely) spoken for a few moments, I asked her where her hearers would go if they died without the Savior. She hesitatingly said, "Hell..." Then she began to weep and added, "...*but God is nice.*"

God is many things—holy, perfect, righteous, loving, good—but there is no biblical foundation for saying that He is "nice." The young lady was nice. She was charming. But to tell sinners that their Creator is "nice" will give the impression that He is "pleasant, sweet, delicate, and agreeable." If that was her image of God, no wonder she was offended by the biblical revelation of His nature. Sometime after that incident, another young lady publicly reproved me for preaching about future punishment. She called out "God loves you... just ask Jesus into your heart right now!" When I asked her where the crowd would go if they died without Jesus Christ she said, "They won't go to heaven." I asked where they would go. She said, "They won't go to be with God." Again I pressed her as to the specific location, and she said, "To a *not very nice* place." Her dilemma was that the mention of hell, without the Law to make it reasonable, made her God look like a tyrant and brought with it the scorn of the world.

Professor Douglas Groothuis of the evangelical Denver Seminary said, "Even some evangelicals, who generally take a more literal approach to biblical teachings, view hell as 'a blemish to be covered up by the cosmetic of divine love'" (*U.S. News & World Report*, January 31, 2000). They deliberately cover over any mention of the cliff toward which the blind man is headed. They don't want to alarm him.

No wonder the world has a misguided understanding of the nature of God. *The Washington Post* (January 9, 2000) put it this way:

> Over the years, Ed and Joanne Liverani have found many reasons to summon God. But now, at middle age, they've boiled it down to one essential: "Not to get clobbered by life."

So sometime in the past ten years the Liveranis began to build their own church, salvaging bits of their old religion that they liked and chucking the rest. The first to go were an angry, vengeful God and hell—"That's just something they say to scare you," Ed said. They kept Jesus, "because Jesus is big on love."

God Hates the Sin

A failure to use the Law lawfully has also forced contemporary evangelism into saying things like "God hates the sin, but loves the sinner." This was used in the late 1990s as what was obviously perceived as an inoffensive way to reach out to homosexuals. It backfired, and resulted instead in Christians being accused of "singling out" the sin of homosexuality—which they had done.

The Bible tells us that the Law was *made* for homosexuals (1 Timothy 1:9,10). Instead of falling into the trap of condemning homosexuals for their sexual preference, we must show them that they are damned *despite* their lifestyle. Many times I have reasoned with homosexuals about their sin, without even addressing the sexual sin that they are so ready to defend. When they understand that they have other **Instead of condemning homosexuals for their sexual preference, we must show them they are damned *despite* their lifestyle.**

sins—lying, stealing, idolatry, covetousness, lust, anger, blasphemy, hatred, etc.—and that they are in danger of damnation, they will see their need to repent and trust in the Savior. Then they will receive a new heart and new desires.

The "God hates the sin and loves the sinner" thought isn't a new concept. Charles Finney wrote in *The Guilt of Sin:*

God is not angry merely against the sin abstracted from the sinner, but against the sinner himself. Some persons have labored hard to set up this ridiculous and absurd abstraction, and would fain make it appear that God is angry at sin, yet not at the sinner. He hates the theft, but loves the thief. "He abhors adultery, but is pleased with the adulterer." Now this is supreme nonsense. The sin has no moral character apart from the sinner. The act is nothing apart from the actor. The very thing that God hates and disapproves is not the mere event—the thing done in distinction from the doer; but it is the *doer himself*. It grieves and displeases Him that a rational moral agent, under His government, should array himself against his own God and Father, against all that is right and just in the universe. This is the thing that offends God. The sinner himself is the direct and the only object of His anger.

So the Bible shows. God is angry with the wicked, not with the abstract sin. If the wicked turn not, God will whet His sword—He hath bent His bow and made it ready—not to shoot at the *sin*, but the *sinner*—the wicked man who has done the abominable thing. This is the only doctrine of either the Bible or of common sense on this subject (Kregel Publications, 1965, reprinted 1985).

CHAPTER 16

The Mystery of the Fish

We are now going to uncover a mystery that had me puzzled for years. Jesus said that the kingdom of God is like a mustard seed that a man put in his garden. It grew and became a large tree and the birds[7] of the air nested in its branches (Luke 13:18,19). Then He said:

> [The kingdom of God] is like leaven, which a woman took and hid in three measures of meal till it was all leavened (v. 21).

This is a little strange, because the children of Israel were commanded to eat only *unleavened* bread (Exodus 12:15–20). Anyone who ate bread that contained leaven was to be "cut off from Israel."

Mark's Gospel records that, not long after Jesus fed the four thousand, the Pharisees came to Him and demanded a sign from heaven. Jesus then told His disciples to beware of the "leaven of the Pharisees and the leaven of Herod" (in Matthew 16:6 He also included the Sadducees). The disciples thought He was chiding them for forgetting to take some bread with them. All they had was one loaf of bread. When they began to wonder why He had spoken of the leaven, Jesus said,

> "Why do you reason because you have no bread? Do you not yet perceive nor understand? Is your heart still

hardened? Having eyes, do you not see? And having ears, do you not hear? And do you not remember? When I broke the five loaves for the five thousand, how many baskets full of fragments did you take up?"

They said to Him, "Twelve." "Also, when I broke the seven for the four thousand, how many large baskets full of fragments did you take up?" And they said, "Seven." So He said to them, "How is it you do not understand?" (Mark 8:17–21).

Why does a man live in hypocrisy? Simply because he has not been humbled by the Law of God.

How could the leftover bread be a key to understanding the leaven of the Pharisees, the Sadducees, and Herod? In Matthew 16:11,12 we are given more light on what "leaven" is:

Then they understood that He did not tell them to beware of the leaven of bread, but of the doctrine of the Pharisees and Sadducees.

If the leaven of the Pharisees and the Sadducees is merely their "doctrine," why was Herod lumped in with them? Again, what has their doctrine got to do with *excess* loaves of bread?

The answer may be in what leaven *does*. It "puffs up." Without leaven, bread lies low. With just a pinch, it exults itself way beyond measure. When Paul spoke of the work of leaven, it was in the context of pride. He said, "Your glorying is not good. Do you not know that a little leaven leavens the whole lump?" (1 Corinthians 5:6).

The self-righteous Pharisee prayed with head held high, puffing out his chest, thanking God that he wasn't like other men. It was pride that caused the Sadducees—the intellectual elite—to deny (even with the light of Scripture) the existence of angels and the resurrection. It was pride that caused Herod to murder the greatest man born of women, rather than back down in front of his honored guests.

Perhaps the reference to the leftover loaves was to remind us that the bedfellow of pride is abundance. Pride is fed by independent wealth, whether it is a wealth of knowledge (which 1 Corinthians 8:1 says "puffs up") or materialism. Independent wealth was the sin of the Laodicean church. They said, "I am rich, have become wealthy, and have need of nothing" (Revelation 3:17). The rich man needed bigger barns, but he wasn't rich in the sight of his God (Luke 12:16–21). He was puffed up with a sense of his own carnal security. He was "high-minded," something that the rich are discouraged from being (1 Timothy 6:17). The proud, self-righteous man thinks that his own good works will save him. He is "puffed up" by his fleshly mind (Colossians 2:18).

In Luke 12:1 we are given further light on "leaven." Jesus said, "Beware of the leaven of the Pharisees, which is hypocrisy." The Sadducees and Herod had this in common: they were hypocrites (Matthew 16:1–3). Herod heard John gladly, and yet he lived in adultery. Why is a man proud, why is he self-righteous, why does he live in hypocrisy? Simply because he has not been humbled by the Law of God. "The perfect Law of liberty" has never been used so that he could see his true state:

> If anyone is a hearer of the word and not a doer, he is like a man observing his natural face in a mirror; for he observes himself, goes away, and immediately forgets what kind of man he was. But he who looks into the perfect law of liberty and continues in it, and is not a forgetful hearer but a doer of the work, this one will be blessed in what he does (James 1:23–25).

Peter's Amazing Ties

Before we look at why leaven was placed in *three* measures of meal, it is relevant to take a look at Peter's close ties to the number three (it would seem that the number three and

Peter are tied in with the evangelistic enterprise):

- Three times the New Testament relates the story of the three disciples on the Mount of Transfiguration, where Peter suggested building three tabernacles.
- In the Garden of Gethsemane, Jesus returned three times to the three disciples. When He addressed them about sleeping while He was praying, He spoke to Peter.
- Three times Peter denied Jesus.
- The "three-time denial" of Peter is mentioned three times in three Gospels.
- Peter was asked three times by Jesus if he loved Him.
- When Peter preached at Pentecost, three thousand were saved.
- When he preached at Pentecost, the Bible makes a point to give the time: it was the "third hour of the day" (Acts 2:15).
- In Acts 11:10, Peter's vision (of the sheet full of animals coming down from heaven), occurred three times.
- When Peter was called to speak to the Gentiles, three men came for him.
- We will now look to John 21:1–14 and see who the Bible speaks of when Jesus appeared to His disciples for the *third time* after the resurrection.

When Peter determined to go and catch some fish, Thomas, Nathanael, James, John, and two other disciples decided that they would go with him. They fished all night and caught nothing. When the morning light came they saw a figure standing on the shore. A voice came from the stranger: "Children, have you any food?" Then He said something similar to words they had heard before: "Cast the net on the right side of the boat, and you will find some." They obeyed and caught so many fish that they couldn't lift the net. Peter said, "It is the Lord!," put on his outer garment, and plunged into the sea. The disciples followed him by boat, dragging the net full of fish.

When they came to land they found that Jesus already had a fire of coals with fish laid on it, and some bread. When He said to bring some of the fish they had just caught, it was Peter who fetched them:

> Simon Peter went up and dragged the net to land, full of large fish, one hundred and fifty-three; and although there were so many, the net was not broken.

Why does the Bible take the time to inform us that there were one hundred and fifty-three fish?

In Luke 5:4–7, when Jesus told Peter to "launch out into the deep and let down your nets for a catch," Peter caught "a great number of fish." The number was so vast that the net began to break. Peter then called for another boat, and when both were loaded, they began to sink under the weight. *That is impressive.*

In the case of the one hundred and fifty-three fish, the net could be dragged, and the weight neither sank the boat nor caused the net to break. Therefore it's safe to assume that Luke's "great number" of fish was more than one hundred and fifty-three. If Scripture is merely informing us of the number to impress the reader (a fisherman's story), it would make sense to inform us of the *larger* number of fish caught in this net-breaking, boat-sinking incident. But in this case, no number is mentioned. Jesus then linked the incident to evangelism by telling Peter, "Do not be afraid. From now on you will catch men" (Luke 5:10).

Because of this, it is reasonable to wonder why we are told that there were *one hundred and fifty-three* fish. However, there is no mention of the number one hundred and fifty-three in any other portion of Scripture to give us a clue. Unless the number is hidden...for some reason. It is.

CHAPTER 17

The Mystery Solved

*I*n the previous chapter, we looked at leaven, Peter, his connection with the number three, and the mystery number one hundred and fifty-three. Let's turn our attention to 2 Kings chapter 1:

Then the king sent to him a captain of fifty with his fifty men. So he went up to him; and there he was, sitting on the top of a hill. And he spoke to him: "Man of God, the king has said, 'Come down!'" So Elijah answered and said to the captain of fifty, "If I am a man of God, then let fire come down from heaven and consume you and your fifty men." And fire came down from heaven and consumed him and his fifty.

Then he sent to him another captain of fifty with his fifty men. And he answered and said to him: "Man of God, thus has the king said, 'Come down quickly!'" So Elijah answered and said to them, "If I am a man of God, let fire come down from heaven and consume you and your fifty men." And the fire of God came down from heaven and consumed him and his fifty.

Again, he sent a third captain of fifty with his fifty men. And the third captain of fifty went up, and came and fell on his knees before Elijah, and pleaded with him, and said to him: "Man of God, please let my life and the life of these fifty servants of yours be precious in your sight. Look, fire has come down from heaven and burned up the first two captains of fifties with their fifties. But let my life now be precious in your sight" (2 Kings 1:9–14).

We are told that fifty men and their captain were sent to arrest Elijah. They were devoured by fire from heaven. Another fifty were commissioned, led by their captain. They too were devoured by fire from heaven. Another fifty men were sent out with their captain. This time the captain "fell on his knees," interceded on their behalf, and saved them from heaven's fire.

A great mass of the contemporary Body of Christ is lukewarm toward the lost, toward prayer, toward God's Word.

Three groups of fifty-one men were sent out. (There again is the number three.) Three times fifty-one is one hundred and fifty-three. *There* is our hidden number. Two-thirds perished by fire. One-third were saved because of the captain's intercession.

There are striking parallels between the Elijah incident and the Church. Those who are saved from Him who is coming "in flaming fire" (2 Thessalonians 1:8) are saved because of the ministry of the Captain of our salvation (Hebrews 2:10). He always lives to make intercession for us (Hebrews 7:25).

Do we have here an indication that two-thirds of those who have professed to be in the Body of Christ down through the ages will hear those terrifying words, "I never knew you; depart from Me, you who practice lawlessness"? Is this an indication that only *one-third* of the professing Church will be saved? One thing I do know is that a great mass of the contemporary Body of Christ is lukewarm toward the lost, toward prayer, toward God's Word. Jesus warned that the lukewarm would be spewed out of His mouth (Revelation 3:16).

God only knows how many will be saved, but after Jesus likened the kingdom of God to leaven, "which a woman took and hid in three measures of meal,"[8] the disciples asked *how many* would be saved. He answered by saying that many will seek to enter in but will not be able (Luke 13:23–27). Then He puts His finger on why. *They were "workers of iniquity"* (v. 27). They were *lawless*, transgressors of the Moral Law. They obviously didn't fear God enough to obey Him.

Again, in light of the one-third saved, two-thirds lost, look at the context of these verses:

> "Strike the Shepherd, and the sheep will be scattered; then I will turn My hand against the little ones. And it shall come to pass in all the land," says the Lord, "that two-thirds in it shall be cut off and die, but one-third shall be left in it: I will bring the one-third through the fire, will refine them as silver is refined, and test them as gold is tested. They will call on my Name, and I will answer them. I will say, "This is My people"; and each one will say, "The Lord is my God" (Zechariah 13:7–9).

There is no question that the Shepherd who is struck is a reference to Jesus (Mark 14:27). It is also clear that these verses can easily be applied to God's dealings with the Church in refining it in fire as gold is tested (1 Peter 1:7). The Church is made up of those who have called upon the name of the Lord (Romans 10:13). God can say of the Church, "This is My people." We were once not a people, but we "are now the people of God" (1 Peter 2:10).

We have a vast multitude waiting within the gospel net, thinking that they are saved, when they don't have the "things that accompany salvation" (Hebrews 6:9). According to Dr. D. James Kennedy, "The vast majority of people who are members of churches in America today are not Christians. I say that without the slightest fear of contradiction. I base it on empirical evidence of twenty-four years of examining thousands of people." Thanks in large part to the methods of modern evangelism, they have named the name of Christ, but have never departed from iniquity (lawlessness). They call Jesus Lord, but do not do the things He tells them. They profess to know Him, but to them He will say, "*I never knew you;* depart from Me, you who practice lawlessness!" (Matthew 7:23, italics added). He will come "in flaming fire taking vengeance on those who do not know God, and on those who do not obey the gospel of our Lord Jesus Christ. These shall be punished with everlasting destruction from the presence of the Lord and from the glory of His power" (2 Thessalonians 1:8,9). Then they will finally know the fear of God.

Stay with me, because we are now going to look at how we can identify these false professions. They seem to have one thing in common...

CHAPTER 18

A Burden for the Lost

*I*n the blackness of Adullam's cave, David longed for a drink of the cool water of Bethlehem's well. Saul hounded him like a mad dog. Dare David risk being seen venturing outside the cave? Yet, his thirst would not subside. He remembered the hot days of his childhood, when his thirst drove him to draw fresh water from the deep well. The more he thought upon it, the more his desire grew, until he broke the silence and whispered, "Oh, that someone would give me a drink of the water from the well of Bethlehem, which is by the gate!" (2 Samuel 23:15).

The Scriptures then tell us: "So the three mighty men broke through the camp of the Philistines, and drew water from the well of Bethlehem that was by the gate, and took it and brought it to David. Nevertheless he would not drink it, but poured it out to the Lord. And he said, 'Far be it from me, O Lord, that I should do this! Is this not the blood of the men who went in jeopardy of their lives?' Therefore he would not drink it. These things were done by the three mighty men" (2 Samuel 23:16,17).

The mighty three had a love for David that was more than lip service, expressed by the fact that they risked their lives merely to get a drink of water for their beloved leader. Yet, David's reaction to their display of love was to pour the water out on the ground as a drink offering to the Lord.

Some may be tempted to say, "Surely, if those men went to such effort to get the water, at least David could have drunk it!" But we have here something far deeper than mere human gratitude. *David's conscience would not allow him to indulge in self-gratification.* He said, "This is the blood of the men who went in jeopardy of their lives!" *How could he drink it?* It was more than just a cup of water. It was an evident token, a symbol, proof of their love and devotion to him. The cost was too great. His only course of action was to give it to God, to pour that precious water out as a drink offering to the Lord.

One Big Gap

Sue was once awakened at 4:00 a.m. to the sound of the blaring television set. She immediately thought that one of our children couldn't sleep and was watching TV. However, it was so loud, she decided she would go downstairs and turn it down.

When she arrived in the den, she found that one of the family dogs had accidentally stood on the remote control and was watching the sports channel.

It fascinates us to see an animal imitate us with a wink or what seems to be a smile, or if it watches the sports channel. However, although evolution tries to link us to animals there is one big gap. As humans, we know that we are "beings." We are aware of our destiny with death. We are aware of the existence of a Supreme Being. God has placed eternity in our hearts.

A non-Christian friend of mine found he had six months to live. His friends told him to spend the last six months doing a "brothel crawl." He wasn't interested. He found that he had something within his heart considerably stronger than his sex drive—it was the will to live. Deep within his heart he had a cry, "Oh, *I don't want to die!*" Eternity was in his heart. Its deep whisper was, "Oh, that one would give me a drink of water from the wells of salvation."

Before the beginning of time, God saw not only the cry of his heart, but the cry within every human heart. The Mighty Three, the Triune God, broke through the hosts of hell to draw water from the Well of Bethlehem. God was in Christ, reconciling the world back to Himself. Now the offer to sinful humanity is: "Whoever drinks of the water that I shall give him will never thirst. But the water that I shall give him will become in him a fountain of water springing up into everlasting life" (John 4:14).

The true convert holds the Cup of Salvation in his trembling hands. He has seen the cost of his redemption. He sees that he was not redeemed with silver or gold, but with the precious Blood of Christ. Like David, he cannot drink of that cup in a spirit of self-indulgence. Rather than drink in the pleasures and the comforts of the Christian life, his reasonable service is to present himself as a living sacrifice, holy and acceptable, and pour his life out as a drink offering to the Lord.

Delightful Heart

I was killing time in a department store when an elderly man struck up a conversation with me. It wasn't long before the conversation swung around to the things of God. When I asked this man if he had a Christian background, his answer was interesting. He said, "Oh, I am a churchgoer. I believe in God the Father; and the Son, *He's around too...somewhere.*" His reply was both humorous and tragic. This man went to church, obviously had faith in God, believed in the deity and the resurrection of Jesus Christ, *yet he was not saved.*

If you love God, your heart will go out to the millions who are in such a state. They are in the "valley of decision." Valleys are often without direct light, and direct light is what sinners need. They don't understand the issues. They are so close to salvation; it is as near as their heart and mouth. Yet without repentance, they will perish. Such thoughts are grievous. If you are born of God's Spirit, you will find that something compels you to run to the lost, to reach out to the unsaved, because God gave you a new heart that delights to do His will.

Well-known author and pastor Oswald Chambers said, "So long as there is a human being who does not know Jesus Christ, I am his debtor to serve him until he does." Bible teacher C. F. W. Walthers said, "A believer is ready to serve everybody wherever he can. He cannot but profess the gospel before men, even though he foresees that he can reap nothing but ridicule and scorn for it; yes, he is ready also to give his life for the gospel."

One cannot help but see Peter's passion for the lost, so evidently portrayed for us in the Book of Acts. He put behind him the three denials of his Lord, and stood before a multitude on the day of Pentecost. When a crowd gathered around the lame man who had been healed, he boldly preached the gospel to them. He testified before the very ones who had murdered the Savior, and he told them so. He had a passion for his God and a passion for sinners.

What was the apostle Paul's greatest passion? This longing, this aspiration, this yearning, *was simply for the salvation of the lost.* His greatest passion was for evangelism, something made evident by his own words. In the introduction of his letter to the Romans, Paul said that he was in debt to the world. His evangelistic zeal was so great that he said he would give up his relationship with Jesus Christ if it would mean that his brethren would be saved. Look at these sobering words:

> I tell the truth in Christ, I am not lying, my conscience also bearing me witness in the Holy Spirit, that I have great sorrow and continual grief in my heart. For I could wish that I myself were accursed from Christ for my

brethren, my countrymen according to the flesh (Romans 9:1–3).

I have looked at a number of Bible commentaries to see what they make of these verses. They have said that Paul could not be speaking of his own salvation. The reference is rather to Paul's willingness to be cut off from Israel. It's my understanding that the apostle was *already* cut off from Israel because of his faith in Jesus. If it was merely a reference to being cut off from his people, why did he say that he had *already* suffered the loss of all things? If they were but rubbish to him, why then does he have to back that up with (what seems like) oaths to make his point?

It is as though Paul was writing to hearers who would not be able to understand such love. How could evangelistic intensity weigh so heavy on a man that he was prepared to be cut off from any association with the Lord Jesus, to see that desire fulfilled? Such a statement could not penetrate selfish minds without a thoughtful preparation. They would not believe him, so Paul testifies that in what he was about to say:

- He is telling the truth in Christ. The very One who was truth itself was Paul's witness that what he was about to say was true.

- His Holy Spirit–regenerated conscience bore witness that he spoke the truth. He had cultivated a conscience that was tender before God and man, and the "work of the Law" did not accuse him of lying. His words could not be dismissed as mere exaggeration, or even hyperbole.

Deep within the soul of this man of God lay a burden—a great sorrow, a continual grief. Horror of horrors—he was saved, but his brethren were not.

Perhaps you do think Paul was lying when he said that his concern for the lost meant more to him than his relationship with Jesus. Maybe he had no fear that all liars would have their part in the lake of fire. Perhaps he had no concern that in bearing false witness, he would transgress the Ninth Commandment, for which Ananias and Sapphira where swiftly struck dead in their crooked tracks. Of course, we can't be the judge as to whether or not Paul was telling the truth in Christ, that his conscience was bearing witness in the Holy Spirit, but there certainly is evidence of his evangelistic priority in his writings.

Moses said a similar thing when he asked that God would cut him out of the book of life, rather than judge Israel.

> **"If sinners will be damned, at least let them leap to hell over our bodies...Let not one go there unwarned and unprayed for."**

In light of these thoughts, I don't know how anyone can call themselves a Christian and not have concern for the lost. Charles Spurgeon said, "Have you no wish for others to be saved? Then you are not saved yourself. Be sure of that." He continued, "The saving of souls, if a man has once gained love to perishing sinners and his blessed Master, will be an all-absorbing passion to him. It will so carry him away, that he will almost forget himself in the saving of others. He will be like the brave fireman, who cares not for the scorch or the heat, so that he may rescue the poor creature on whom true humanity has set its heart. If sinners will be damned, at least let them leap to hell over our bodies. And if they will perish, let them perish with our arms about their knees, imploring them to stay. If hell must be filled, at least let it be filled in the teeth of our exertions, and let not one go there unwarned and unprayed for."

When an emergency vehicle drives through a city, the law demands that every other vehicle must pull over and stop. Why? *Because someone's life may be in jeopardy.* It is to be given great priority. That's how we should be when it comes to the eternal salvation of men and women. There is an extreme emergency. *Everything* else must come to a standstill, or we are in danger of transgressing the Moral Law, which demands "You shall love your neighbor as yourself."

Hell should be so real to us that its flames burn away apathy and motivate us to warn the lost. Do we see the unsaved as hell's future fuel? Do we understand that sinful humanity is the anvil of the justice of God? Have we ever been horrified or wept because we fear their fate? The depth of our evangelistic zeal will be in direct proportion to the love we have. If you are not concerned about your neighbor's salvation, then I am concerned for yours.

The evangelistic zeal described on the previous pages should characterize a normal, biblical Christian. However, according to the *Dallas Morning News* (June 11, 1994), sixty-eight percent of professing Christians outside of the "Bible Belt" don't see evangelism as being the number-one priority of the Church. Also in 1994, the Barna Research Group found that among American adults who said that they were "born again," seventy-five percent couldn't even define the Great Commission. A survey by *Christianity Today* (a major evangelistic magazine) found that only one percent of their readership said they had witnessed to someone "recently." That means ninety-nine percent of their readership were just "lukewarm" when it came to concern for the fate of the ungodly. According to *Zondervan Church Source*, ninety-seven percent of the Church has no involvement in any sort of evangelism. Only once in Scripture did Jesus give three parables in a row (Luke chapter 15). He did so to illustrate God's profound concern for the lost soul.

How is it that so many who are within the Church can profess to love God, yet neglect or even *despise* evangelism? The answer is frightening.

CHAPTER 19

The Rich Man

S ome years ago, I read the story that Jesus told of "Lazarus and the Rich Man," and interpreted it in a radically different slant than most. In fact, I have searched many commentaries, and haven't found even one with the same interpretation. I submitted it to seven godly men. Six passed it as being biblically sound. The seventh wasn't too sure. I submit it to you for your consideration.

"There was a certain rich man who was clothed in purple and fine linen and fared sumptuously every day. But there was a certain beggar named Lazarus, full of sores, who was laid at his gate, desiring to be fed with the crumbs which fell from the rich man's table. More-over the dogs came and licked his sores.

"So it was that the beggar died, and was carried by the angels to Abraham's bosom. The rich man also died and was buried.

"And being in torments in [hell], he lifted up his eyes and saw Abraham afar off, and Lazarus in his bosom. Then he cried and said, 'Father Abraham, have mercy on me, and send Lazarus that he may dip the tip of his finger in water and cool my tongue; for I am tormented in this flame.'

"But Abraham said, 'Son, remember that in your lifetime you received your good things, and likewise Lazarus evil things; but now he is comforted and you are tor-

149

mented. And besides all this, between us and you there is a great gulf fixed, so that those who want to pass from here to you cannot, nor can those from there pass to us.'

"Then he said, 'I beg you therefore, father, that you would send him to my father's house, for I have five brothers, that he may testify to them, lest they also come to this place of torment.'

"Abraham said to him, 'They have Moses and the prophets; let them hear them.' And he said, 'No, father Abraham; but if one goes to them from the dead, they will repent.' But he said to him, 'If they do not hear Moses and the prophets, neither will they be persuaded though one rise from the dead'" (Luke 16:19–31).

Is this a picture of the way of salvation? If it is, then it's totally inconsistent with every other biblical reference to deliverance from death. Those who would seek to justify good works as a means of entrance into heaven could find adequate evidence here. Let's look at the passage in the light of such a thought.

First, what was the rich man's sin? Obviously, it was failure to feed Lazarus. If that is the case, then he could have *earned* salvation. If a non-Christian wanted to earn his way into heaven, should he then give food to the homeless? How much food would merit eternal life? No, since salvation is "by grace [divine influence]...through faith...not of works" (Ephesians 2:8,9), the rich man's sin could not have been a mere failure to give Lazarus free food.

Perhaps his sin was the fact that he was rich. Then Abraham should have been damned, for he was rich. Was gluttony the rich man's sin? Not necessarily. According to *Vine's Expository Dictionary of New Testament Words*, "sumptuously" means "goodly."

Why the reference to his clothing? Was his apparel or the color of it abhorrent to God?

Second, what did Lazarus do to merit salvation? Did his

suffering in this life appease the wrath of God, and gain him entrance into the next? If so, then let us seek suffering instead of the Savior. Let us inflict our bodies as did the prophets of Baal, or crawl up the steps of some cold cathedral until blood pours from festered wounds, then call for the dogs to lick them. If this is a picture of the way of salvation, then eternal justice can be perverted, God can be bribed, and the sacrifice of the wicked is not an abomination to the Lord.

The story therefore *must* have another meaning.

Who is the Rich Man?

Let us establish several principles of biblical interpretation that will help us unlock the meaning of the story of Lazarus and the rich man.

- Purple is the biblical color of royalty (Esther 8:15).
- Fine linen represents the righteousness of the saints (Revelation 19:8).
- The Church is referred to as the "royal priesthood" (1 Peter 2:9).
- The tabernacle (a type of the Church) was made up of fine linen and purple (Exodus 26:1).

The rich man is a type of the *professing* Church, and the leper (which is what most Bible commentators agree he was) is a type of the sinner.

The foul sores of sin permeate his very being. He is as "an unclean thing." His righteousnesses are like filthy, leprous rags. Those who touch him are commanded to "hate even the garment defiled by the flesh" (Jude 23). Unclean spirits, like hungry dogs, feed off the wounds of his sin, waiting to consume him at death. He is laid at the gate of the Church —that rich, fat Laodicean Church...the "royal priesthood" of believers, clothed in fine linen and purple, faring sumptuously on the teachings of prayer, prophecy, providence, justification, sanctification, and purification. This Church enjoys an "abundant life" of men's camps, youth camps, marriage seminars, ladies meetings, worship, prayer, and praise; young people's meetings, Bible studies, audiotapes, videotapes, and CDs; it heaps to itself teachers, having "itching ears"…ears so scratched by feasting, so dulled by overconsumption, *that the muffled cries of Lazarus at the gate go unheeded!*

We have become like Israel when God spoke to them in their prosperity, but they said, "I will not hear" (Jeremiah 22:21). The sin of the Church isn't that it's rich, *but that it hasn't the compassion to throw even a few evangelistic crumbs to starving sinners at the gate.*

The rich man's thoughts are only for himself. He is filled with his own ways. We have built for ourselves big beautiful buildings, with cool clear acoustics and colorful carpets, where as cozy Christians we sit on padded pews, living in luxury while sinners sink into hell. We say that we are rich, but we are poor, blind, wretched, miserable, and naked. I thank God for comfortable pews and quality sound systems, *but not at the cost of neglecting the lost.* We have lavished luxury on the lifeboat, while people drown en masse around us.

I have watched vast multitudes crowd around ministries of "power," "healing," and "faith," and prayed that what I suspect is untrue. I have listened to the message that these men and women bring and hoped that I was mistaken in my thought that there was something radically wrong. I'm not bothered by what they say, *but by what is left unsaid.* There is healing in the atonement (who doesn't pray that God would heal a sick loved one?); we *need* to have faith in God's promises; and historically God does bless His people and lift them out of poverty, hunger, and suffering. *But why don't these ministers preach Christ crucified for the sins of the world?* They consistently leave the cross out of their message, other than to mention it as the means of purchasing healing and prosperity for God's people. Why is there no preaching against sin, and exalting God's righteousness?

I look at the vast seas of people before them and think to myself that there must be many who don't know God's mercy in Christ, yet they are not warned to flee from the wrath to come. Judgment Day isn't mentioned, neither is hell, nor is there a call to repentance. I try to be gracious and excuse them by thinking that perhaps these are "teachers" within the Body of Christ, whose particular gifting is to exhort and encourage rather than to seek to save what is lost. However, the most gifted of teachers cannot be excused for not caring about the fate of the ungodly. The apostle Paul was the greatest of teachers, yet he pleaded for prayer that he would share the gospel with boldness as he "ought to speak." He said, "Woe is me if I do not preach the gospel!" (1 Corinthians 9:16). What are the ethical implications of a fire captain who is preoccupied with making sure that his firemen are well-dressed, while people he is supposed to be saving burn to death?

I pray that the following letter I received doesn't represent the throngs who are followers of these men and women. I tremble when I suspect that it does:

> I don't think I've thanked you lately for waking me out of my false conversion. Please don't let discouragement ever hinder you from continuing to preach "Hell's Best Kept Secret." I believe it's the perfect message to wake up anyone regardless of their denomination...*I never, ever thought the day would come that I would call myself an ex–"Word of Faith"er.* If Paul was a Hebrew of Hebrews, I was a faith guy of faith guys. A card-carrying, tape-listening-to, TV-preacher-watching, book-reading, seminar-attending, positive-confessing faith guy was I. And it was all a waste of time. I write this to show you that if one who was as extreme as myself can be snatched from such a slumber, I believe anyone with an ounce of self-honesty is a candidate for this wake-up call. Not that I am

any more opposed to the errors of Word of Faith doctrine than those of others in contemporary Christendom, but it's what I'm most familiar with. Like any of them, its greatest error is that it's a broad way and a wide gate.

If the Prodigal Son had returned to his father *before* he realized that his desires were base, he may have come to him with a different attitude. Instead of seeing that his desires were for pig food and saying, "Father I have sinned...make me like one of your hired servants," he may have said, "Father, I have run out of money." Rather than saying, "*Make* me," he would say, "*Give* me." Instead of wanting to serve his father, his father would become his servant. That is the category of many who sit in the midst of the Body of Christ. The Law has not been used to show them that their sinful desires are *exceedingly* sinful. God is merely a means to further their own ends.

Admirers of the Admiral

Few see how great a sin it is to neglect evangelism, because so few have any concern for the lost. Many within the Church think we are here to worship the Lord, and evangelism is for the few who have that gift. Their call to worship is a higher calling.

There was once a respectable captain of a ship whose crew spoke highly of him. They said they esteemed him to a point where everyone knew of their professed love for him.

One day, however, the captain saw to his horror that an ocean liner had struck an iceberg and people were drowning in the freezing water ahead of his ship. He quickly directed his vessel to the area, stood on the bridge, and made an impassioned plea to his crew to throw out the life preservers. But instead of obeying his charge, the crew lifted their hands and said, "Praise the captain...praise you...we love you! You are worthy of our praise."

Can you see that the reality of their adoration *should have been seen by their obedience to his command?* Their "admiration" was nothing but empty words.

If we worship in spirit, we will also worship in truth. To lift our hands in adoration *to* God, yet refuse to reach out our hands in evangelism *for* God is nothing but empty hypocrisy. "You shall worship the Lord your God, *and Him only you shall serve*" (Matthew 4:10, italics added) is more than a mere satanic rebuke. If the average church made as much noise *about* God on Monday as it does *to* God on Sunday, we would have revival.

To lift our hands in adoration *to* God, yet refuse to reach out our hands in evangelism *for* God is nothing but empty hypocrisy.

Yet, in his book *The Coming Revival*, Bill Bright reports that "only two percent of believers in America regularly share their faith in Christ with others" (New*Life* Publications, p. 65).

Evangelist Bill Fay has spoken at more than 1,500 conferences and churches. At each meeting, he would ask how many had shared their faith in the previous year. Never once did he find a church where more than ten percent raised their hands. In December 1999, at a church of nearly 4,000 in Southern California, he found that only 12 had shared their faith in the previous year. Early in 2000, a Southern Baptist publication called *The Gatekeeper* revealed that ninety-seven percent of their membership will go to their graves without sharing their faith. Evangelism should be the life's breath of the Body of Christ. If the breath is not in the body, neither is the life.

This lack of concern for the lost may be because Christians haven't been taught the biblical priority of evangelism —even though it is so evident in Scripture. However, if we are aware of our debt to both Jew and Gentile, and yet refuse to hold out the Bread of Life, we prove to be the rich man of whom Jesus spoke.

I have always maintained that the very reason the Church exists on earth is to evangelize the world—to be a light in darkness, to preach the gospel to every creature. If we worship God, yet ignore His command to take the gospel to every creature, then our worship is in vain. It is to draw near to Him with our lips, but to have our hearts far from Him. I have often said that if you want to find the "evangelism" section in your local Christian bookstore, you had better take your magnifying glass. This is not the fault of the store, but is just an indication of where the modern church's priorities lie.

With this concern in mind, I wrote a book calling Christians back to evangelism, and sent the manuscript to an organization to review it. If they think the book has potential, they forward it to a publisher. This is what the reviewer said:

> I like the content of this manuscript very much. It contains a much-needed message for Christians about the Great Commission. Nevertheless, I see a serious problem when it comes to marketing this material. In order for a book to be marketed successfully in the bookstores, its identity must be clear. Where does this book go in the store? Is it a devotional book? Or a Bible study manual? Or is it an inspirational, "Christian living" book?

They rejected it on that basis. Despite this being a "much-needed message," they think the "serious problem" lies not in the Church itself but in the marketability of the message.

The Evangelical Enterprise

One of America's most positively popular preachers once made a crystal clear statement that revealed his priorities. He said, "I don't think anything has been done in the name of Christ and under the banner of Christianity that has proven more destructive to human personality and hence counter-productive to the evangelism enterprise than the often crude, uncouth, and un-Christian strategy of attempting to make people aware of their lost and sinful condition."

What then does he consider to be the "evangelism enterprise" if it's not to warn sinners to flee from the wrath to come? It is clear what the problem is. Modern Christianity has degenerated into merely a means of self-improvement, self-esteem, and self-indulgence. It is self-centered rather than centered on and in the will of God. The same preacher reveals the cause of his error by saying, "The Ten Commandments were designed to put pride and dignity in your life." *That's not what the Bible teaches.* The Ten Commandments were given to do the exact opposite: to humble us. They show us that sin is "exceedingly sinful," and that we are in *desperate* need of God's mercy. The Bible tells us that the "Law brings about wrath" (Romans 4:15). It shows us the reality of God's wrath abiding on us. It is God's purpose for us to use the Commandments lawfully—to make people aware of their lost and sinful condition, "crude and uncouth" though it may seem to some.

In Luke 16:19, the rich man's problem was that he was idolatrous. His understanding of God was wrong. He lacked the knowledge of God, and therefore he didn't fear God, and because he didn't fear God, he didn't obey Him. He didn't love his neighbor as himself. Lazarus was starving at his gate, and he couldn't care less.

The irony of the story of the rich man was that he waited until he was in hell before he became concerned for others.

CHAPTER 20

Whose Cookies?

f you witness regularly, you will know that many in contemporary America think they are good people. This is the fruit of a nation that has forsaken God's Law. The Law is "good," but when there is no knowledge of the Law, "good" becomes subjective. This was the case with the rich young ruler's question, "Good Teacher, what good thing shall I do that I may have eternal life?" (Matthew 19:16). Jesus reproved his misuse of the word "good." The young man was one who used the word without knowledge of its true meaning.

Sinners often say similar things. An athlete may say that "the good Man upstairs" helped him win a race. Or they seek to justify their sin by saying, "You're a good person; tell me why the Bible says..." This is why I find it frustrating when I do a good deed for someone who doesn't know that I am a Christian. If I help push a car, for example, I don't want them to think, "I knew there were still good people. That restores my faith in human nature." Often, the more "good" people the world can find, the more they will try to justify their own goodness and reject God's mercy. Like the rich young ruler, they need to be enlightened as to what *good* is. The way to do this is to follow the example of Jesus and decimate the fig leaves of self-righteousness with the Ten Cannons of God's Law.

A famous Rogers and Hammerstein musical contained the words, "Somewhere in my childhood, I must have done something good." The young lady who was singing the song had fallen in love and was brimming with happiness. It was her way of saying that God was rewarding her with the blessing of true love because she merited it. While God does reward good and evil, her words exemplify the world's erroneous philosophy. Any good that comes our way doesn't solely come to us because *we* have done something good, but because God is good. Until we understand that "there is none who does good, no, not one," we will expect blessings because we think we are good and therefore deserve them. When life brings us suffering, we become angry at God because we think God owes us happiness.

An unregenerate world judges God as being the guilty party for the sufferings of humanity.

The Law not only gives us understanding of the grace of the cross, but of the grace of life itself—that He has not dealt with us according to our iniquities. The only thing God "owes" us is wrath.

A man in a London airport decided to purchase some English butter cookies. He opened the small tin, took one out then placed the tin at his feet. After he had waited for his flight for some time, a middle-aged woman smiled politely and sat next to him. To his astonishment, without a word of permission she reached down, took a cookie out of the tin, and ate it. He couldn't believe what this complete stranger had just done! Suspecting that it may be a local custom, he smiled at her and took one himself. A few minutes later, she took another one. He smiled awkwardly and took a second cookie himself. She then took a third. *Who did this woman think she was?* Then she took the very last cookie, looked at him, broke it in half and offered it to him. *The audacity of the woman!* Other words such as "brazen," "rude," "impudent," and "presumptuous" flashed through his mind.

As he was about to express his thoughts, he bent down and saw that his identical tin of cookies was still at his feet. In an instant, he realized that *he* had been the brazen, rude, impudent, and presumptuous person. *He had been eating the cookies of a complete stranger!* He also realized how her response to his actions had in truth been very gracious.

An unregenerate world judges God as being the guilty party for the sufferings of humanity. As far as they are concerned, He is unjust. But the Law of God gives us sudden light to our misconception. It shows us who is eating whose cookies. *We* are the ones who are in transgression. It dawns on us that we are *more* than brazenly impudent in our accusations. We are guilty criminals standing before an unspeakably holy and gracious Judge, accusing Him of transgression. In light of God's holiness, it is hard to understand why He continues to let a sinful humanity such as us even draw another breath.

Facial Injuries

In March 1993, Sue and I were involved in a head-on collision. Fortunately, we sustained only minor head injuries. I was on my way back from the bathroom in the early hours of the morning when Sue got out of my side of the bed. For some reason she looked down for a second and we collided head-on, leaving us both with a fat lip. She presumed that I would see her in the dark, but I was coming from a bright light into a blackened room. I couldn't see a thing.

To presume that the unregenerate man already has the necessary light to be saved is to have a head-on collision with the many Scriptures asserting that there *is none* who understands (Psalm 53:2,3; Romans 3:11,12; 8:7). If we *adulterate* the Word of God by making the Law invalid in its lawful use of bringing light to the sinner, we will have *adul-*

terous converts. Their hearts will love the world and the things in the world. But as we "teach all nations" and, like the disciples, do not cease "teaching and preaching Jesus as the Christ," we will see sinners come to "know His will, and approve the things that are excellent, *being instructed out of the Law*" (Romans 2:18, italics added). "Instructed out of the Law" suggests more than a casual reference to the Ten Commandments. It means to rightly divide the Word of Truth, as a father at the head of a table would break up bread for his children. Charles Spurgeon, in lecturing his students on evangelism, said, "Explain the Ten Commandments and obey the Divine injunction; 'Show my people their transgressions, and the house of Jacob their sins.' Open up the spirituality of the Law as our Lord did."

Sinning Converts

The direct result of the Church being confronted with biblical teaching on true and false conversion would be that the "sinning convert" would no longer be consoled in his sins. Instead of dealing with the symptoms of his non-accountability lifestyle—his fornication, pornography, lack of discipline, lack of holiness, theft, wife beating, adultery, drunkenness, lying, hatred, rebellion, greed, etc.—the pastor would deal with the *cause*. He would say, "A good tree *cannot* bear bad fruit," and "no spring yields both salt water and fresh." He would gently inform his hearer, "It sounds as though you have had a spurious conversion and you need to repent of your lawless deeds and make Jesus Christ your Lord." Then, using the Law of God, he should show the "exceeding sinfulness" of sin and the unspeakable gift of the cross. This should awaken a false convert, put most Christian psychologists out of business, and cut "counseling" to a minimum.

A clear understanding of the reality of true and false conversion would give light to church leaders who are horrified at the state of what they see as the "Church." One respected leader said:

> In survey after survey, researchers find that the life-styles of born-again Christians are virtually indistin-guishable from those of nonbelievers. The divorce rate among Christians is identical to that of nonbelievers. Christian teens are almost as sexually active as non-Christian teens. Pornography, materialism, gluttony, lust, covetousness, and even disbelief are commonplace in many of our churches.

Such teaching would also stop the insanity of modern evangelism's zeal without knowledge, by showing that the category of lukewarm "converts" doesn't exist. There is no division in the kingdom of God for those who are tepid. We should be either hot and stimulating or cold and refreshing. Lukewarm "converts" are not part of the Body of Christ; they merely weigh heavy within the stomach of His Body until He vomits them out of His mouth on the Day of Judgment (Revelation 3:16). They didn't pass through the jagged-edged teeth of the Law of God. They remain hard and impenitent; they were never broken by the Law that they might be absorbed into the bloodstream of the Body of Christ, to become His hands, His feet, and His mouth. They never felt the heartbeat of God, so their hands didn't reach out in com-passion to the lost, their feet were not shod with the prepara-tion of the gospel of peace, and their mouths didn't preach the gospel to every creature. This mass of converts are like the "backslider in heart," who is "filled with his own ways" rather than the ways of God. Their "Here I am Lord, *send him*," doesn't come from a rational fear of man, but from rebellion to the revealed will of the God they call Lord and Master.

Elisha told his servants to make some stew. However, "one went out into the field to gather herbs, and found a wild vine, and gathered from it a lapful of wild gourds, and came and sliced them into the pot of stew, though they did not know what they were." When the stew was being eaten, the guests cried out, "Man of God, there is death in the pot!" Elisha then put flour into the mixture, and "there was nothing harmful in the pot" (2 Kings 4:38–41).

The servants of the Lord have gone into the field of the world and brought back the wild vine of the modern gospel, which they added to the Church. Now there is death in the pot. What should give life-sustaining nourishment instead leads to death. As sinners are fed a gospel poisoned by modern evangelism, they are consuming a deadly mixture and becoming false converts.

The answer is to add flour. Flour is created by going through the process of brokenness; it has been ground to powder. The Law is the millstone that does that most necessary task.

The Wide Gate

In Matthew 7:13,14, Jesus said, "Enter by the narrow gate; for wide is the gate and broad is the way that leads to destruction, and there are many who go in by it. Because narrow is the gate and difficult is the way which leads to life, and there are few who find it."

Jesus warned that the way that leads to destruction was broad. But more than that, He said it had a "gate," and that "many" would "go in" that way. If the way of destruction is the way of the world, which is the usual interpretation, why did Jesus call it a "gate" that many would "enter"? Surely if that were the case, He would have said that the ungodly are *born* into the way of destruction. This thought is supported by the conjunction Jesus used to join verses 13 and 14. He said that the way of destruction is broad and many will enter into it *because* the way that leads to life is narrow. There are only two gates: if they don't go through the narrow, then they will end up going through the broad. He said the wide gate is entered *because* the other gate is narrow.

It seems rather that Jesus, in His usual consistency, is speaking of true and false conversions as He did in the Parable of the Sower, the Wise and Foolish Virgins, the Wheat and Tares, the Good and Bad Fish, the Goats and Sheep, and the Wise and Foolish House Builders. He again uses the word "many" here in describing them, as He did when speaking of the "workers of lawlessness" He never knew (Matthew 7:22,23).

Remember to what Jesus likened the kingdom of God? He said, "It is like a man going to a far country, who left his house and gave authority to his servants, and to each his work, and commanded the doorkeeper to watch" (Mark 13:34). The doorkeeper should keep the door. He should "watch," to allow in only those who should enter. Instead, we have forsaken our watch.

Acceptable Fodder

Again, the false convert is like the Prodigal Son *before* he understood that his appetites were base, that he had "sinned against heaven" and in his father's sight. Because modern evangelism fails to show him heaven's holy standard, he doesn't see that his sin is against God, so he thinks it is quite acceptable to desire "pig food." He returns to his father, but his heart is still with the harlots. He chooses to be with the people of God, and to secretly enjoy the pleasures of sin for a season. He also finds it easier to lie (white lies) than to speak the truth, easier to steal (white-collar crime) than to pay for something, easier to lust than be holy, easier to live for himself than for others, easier to feed his mind on the things of the world rather than the things of God.

The professing convert's mind is on the things of the flesh *because he is still "bound by iniquity,"* as was Simon the sorcerer (Acts 8:23). Like Simon, he may believe, associate with the apostles, and see the miracles of God. He may pass through the waters of baptism and impress many with his subtle trickery, but those who understand the Parable of the Sower and its broad implications are not swayed. They see beyond his sleight-of-hand illusion into reality. They can see, to their horror, that the Church by preaching a Lawless gospel is ushering multitudes through hell's broad gate...a gate that is oiled smooth by modern evangelism.

Nehemiah chose two men to be in charge of gathering citizens for Jerusalem. Their names were Hanani, which means *gracious*, and Hananiah, which means *Jah (Jehovah) has favored*. Scripture tells us that Hananiah was faithful and that he feared God. This was what Nehemiah charged them: "Do not let the gates of Jerusalem be opened until the sun is hot" (Nehemiah 7:2,3). God has favored humanity with the gospel of grace. Those faithful servants who fear God will seek citizens for the New Jerusalem, and they will not open the gates until the sun is hot. They will let the heat of the Law do its most necessary work.

CHAPTER 21

Raiders of the *Contents* of the Lost Ark

*A*s I sat in my car, I really did expect to receive a punch in the face. I had screened a series of television advertisements, warning of rock music that advocated violence and murder. One of the groups that stirred me to do so was called "The Dead Kennedys." The lyrics to one of their songs went:

> I kill children. I love to watch them die. I kill children, make their mommas cry. Crush them under my car, I love to hear them scream. Feed them poison candy, spoil their Halloween.

The advertisements had caused me to wonder if I would get my face rearranged by someone who didn't like what I had done. Now a gentleman in his forties, with a clenched fist and a determined look on his face, was making his way toward my car.

As he approached the open window of my vehicle, he looked me in the eye and asked, "Are you Ray Comfort?" I meekly said that I was. Then, without saying a word, he lifted his large clenched fist, thrust it toward me through the window,...*and dropped $20 in my lap.* Then he walked off without a word.

It would seem that God delights in bringing victory out of what appear to be disastrous situations. Israel stood at the Red Sea, trapped, with no possible way of escape. Then God did the impossible. He brought victory out of what seemed to be a sure fist in the face. Daniel found himself in a pit of ferocious lions. Once again, God brought victory in the face of what appeared to be a devastating situation. Jesus of Nazareth had been crucified. The disciples had been scattered. It seemed that the body had been stolen. *How much darker could life become?* It was then that God revealed the brilliant light of the resurrection. He brought the ultimate victory out of the ultimate disaster.

Criminal Moral Code

In 1983 in Bogota, Colombia, a mother rushed Jensen, her 10-month-old baby who had an acute case of diarrhea, to a hospital near her village. When she came to get her baby the next day, his eyes were bandaged and he was covered with splotches of blood. Horrified, she asked what was wrong with the boy, and was coldly dismissed by a doctor who told her that the child was dying.

In a panic, she raced Jensen to another doctor who examined his wounds and said, "They've stolen his eyes!"

The baby was the victim of "organ-napping," where eyes are removed and the corneas sold on the black market. In one sense Jensen was fortunate—most victims are murdered.

In 1980, when the Ten Commandments were removed from the schools of the United States, the eyes of an entire generation were removed. The "Commandment is a lamp, and the Law a light" (Proverbs 6:23), and removal of the Law left a generation in the dark as to moral absolutes. We now live at a time when a breed of human beings can kill, steal, hate, dishonor their parents, and revile God without qualms of conscience.

In June 1993, six teenage gang members in northwest Houston raped and killed two girls ages 14 and 16. The leader of the gang, Peter Cantu (age 19), boasted how he and other members abducted the two young girls, raped and sodomized them before strangling them. According to their testimony, "It took a while for them to die." They kicked one girl in the mouth with a steel boot, knocking out three of her teeth, then strangled her with a belt until it broke. They strangled the other girl with a shoelace. Then they took turns stomping on their necks to make sure they died. These heinous crimes are all too common in our lawless society.

Today's generation doesn't just lack the moral values of its grandparents; it doesn't have *any* moral values. In previous years, there was a "moral" code even among criminals, that when you stole from someone, you didn't blast him with your gun as you left. This is not so nowadays. We are daily reminded that what one generation permits the next embraces as normality. Years ago, a woman would hesitate to walk in front of a group of men for a concern that they would undress her with their eyes. Nowadays, her fear is that she will be viciously raped, sodomized, and murdered.

In light of the statistics we looked at in the beginning of this book, it would seem that the enemy has removed from the Body of Christ its ability to be salt and light in a dark and decaying world. Jesus warned that if salt lost its flavor, it would be good for nothing except to be trampled underfoot by men. This is why so many hold the Church in contempt. The world has trampled us underfoot, and is reaping terrible consequences.

We are living in times of gross darkness, but remember, this is not a "God-forsaken" world—it is a world that has forsaken God. He can, in His great sovereignty, open Satan's clenched fist and drop the riches of revival in the lap of the Church. Eric W. Hayden, in his book *Spurgeon on Revival*, wrote, "Almost every book dealing with spiritual awakening or a revival of history begins by describing the pre-revival situation in approximately the same words. For instance, you will read such words as these: 'The darkness before the dawn'; 'The sleep of midnight and gross darkness'; or 'disso-

lution and decay.' W. T. Stead, who was a child of the Welsh
Revival of 1859, when writing of the later revival in the
twentieth century, said of it: 'Note how invariably the revival
is preceded by a period of corruption.'"

There is great hope for the masses of false converts who
sit within the Church. It is a rich field
of evangelistic endeavor. The fact that
they are still there is a testimony to the
fact that they remain open to the things
of God. History shows us that virtually
every major revival of the past has
been birthed out of a great awakening
of those who thought they were saved,
but were not. I have seen this teaching
awaken many false converts as to their
true state. God has soundly saved them,
and from there they have begun to be
the witnesses they are commanded to be.

Virtually every major revival has been birthed out of a great awakening of those who thought they were saved, but were not.

Enemy Attack

In closing, let me share with you some insightful words from
Martin Luther. When speaking of using the Law as a schoolmaster to bring sinners to Christ, he said, "This now is the
Christian teaching and preaching, which God be praised, we
know and possess, and it is not necessary at present to devel-
op it further, but only to offer the admonition that it be
maintained in Christendom with all diligence. *For Satan has
attacked it hard and strong from the beginning until present, and
gladly would he completely extinguish it and tread it underfoot*"
(italics added).

The enemy has duped the Church into believing that it is
advancing by getting decisions for Christ. What has actually
happened is that he has invaded our ranks and stripped the
gospel of its power. The ark has been raided.

John Wesley said to those who forsook the Law in its

capacity to prepare the heart for grace:

> O take knowledge what Satan hath gained over thee;
> and, for the time to come, never think or speak lightly of,
> much less dress up as a scarecrow, this blessed instrument
> of the grace of God. Yea, love and value it for the sake of
> Him from whom it came, and of Him to whom it leads.
> Let it be thy glory and joy, next to the cross of Christ.
> Declare its praise, and make it honorable before all men.

I know that his words are true. The enemy hates this
teaching. I have many examples of the enemy's resistance,
but one stands out in my mind. For years as I spoke on this
subject, we tried to get a master audiotape of this teaching so
we could share it with others. Each time we listened to the
tape, we would find a mysterious "buzz" running through it,
or a fifteen-second silence in the middle of an important
illustration. However, in the late nineties, I spoke at a large
church in Chicago that had a sophisticated sound system.
They gave me a one-hour audio master with no flaws on the
entire tape. That is, except for an eight-word sentence that
had to be removed because it was cut in half when the sound
man turned over the tape. That eight-word sentence that had
to be deleted from a one-hour teaching was: "Satan doesn't
want you to hear this teaching."

The devil is quite happy if the Church sings of the power
of the presence of God. But remember that in the Old
Testament, the ark of the covenant signified His presence. It
wasn't the ark that God prized; it was what the ark *contained*.
Have you ever wondered why it was that God manifested
Himself in such a glorious way that the priests in the house
of the Lord could not minister (1 Kings 8:10,11)? It happened when the priests brought in the ark of the covenant.
Scripture tells what was in the ark:

> Nothing was in the ark except the two tablets of
> stone which Moses put there at Horeb (v. 9).

It seems God so esteems His Law that He could not withhold His glorious presence from the temple. The psalmist didn't say, "Oh, how I love Your *ark!*" Paul didn't say, "I delight in the *ark* of God." It was God's holy Law that they loved and revered. That Law was written with the finger of God. It was an expression of His character. We (as individuals and as the Church) are the "temple of the Lord," and when we give the Moral Law its rightful place, perhaps we will truly see that power of His presence—something that causes demons to tremble.

Satan hates this teaching for a number of other reasons. It awakens the false convert to his true state. It puts the fear of God in the heart of the Christian and therefore assists him to walk in holiness. It gives him a *reason* to reach out to the lost. The issue isn't the happiness of sinners in this life, but their eternal welfare in the light of a wrath-filled Creator.

The following letter is typical of how the Law does its wonderful work:

> I am 53 years old. Have committed all sins. I was baptized and saved by God's grace...or so I thought. Have long sensed something wrong. Last week my wife picked up a free cassette tape placed at the cash register of a local sandwich shop. The tape was "Hell's Best Kept Secret." I played the tape as soon as my wife gave it to me. Bingo! I immediately understood what was wrong. I had not been brought to salvation by the Law. At the same time [I realized] that evangelizing is what I am to do...I play HBKS daily and have lost count of how many times I have listened to it. God has my heart. I have absolute faith, a Bible, a box and lots of open air. Anxious for your reply.

The enemy has attacked the use of the Law in evangelism "hard and strong from the beginning until present." However, our great consolation is the fact that this is *God's* teaching, and I believe that it is His timing to bring it to light.

At the risk of sounding melodramatic, I would ask you to consider reading this book again, simply because experience has taught me that its truths will soon be snatched from your mind...unless you make a concerted effort to let them sink deep into the soil of your heart.

It was A. W. Pink who said, "It is true that [many] are praying for worldwide revival. But it would be more timely, and more scriptural, for prayer to be made to the Lord of the Harvest, that He would raise up and thrust forth laborers who would fearlessly and faithfully preach those truths which are calculated to bring about a revival." I firmly believe that the use of the Law in evangelism is one of those truths, and if we want to see a great harvest of souls in these last days, we must hold onto this truth with unwavering conviction.

Do you remember King David's experience with the ark (2 Samuel 6:3–8)? Instead of having the sons of Kohath carry it on poles as the Scriptures commanded, he put it on an ox cart. As the ark was brought into Israel, the ox stumbled and it began to rock. When Uzzah reached out his hand to steady it, God killed him. R. C. Sproul rightly said that Uzzah presumed his hand was cleaner than the dirt.

We have put the ark of the gospel on the ox cart of modern evangelism. Sincere though we may have been, we dare not presume that we can reach out our sinful hand and steady the things of God, and then carry on the way we have been going.

If we fear our Creator, we must discard our own ways, and then do all things according to the pattern given to us in Holy Scripture.

Thank you for being open-minded and allowing me to share my heart with you. May God continue to bless you and grant you your heart's deepest desires, as you delight yourself in Him.

■ ■ ■

If you have been appreciative of this teaching, you may like to obtain a two-video series called "The Premiere Series," which expounds the message of this book. The series was produced for television and includes a study guide. We also have a very popular sixteen-audiotape series called "Hell's Best Kept Secret." When you purchase this series for U.S. $49.95, we will give you five of Ray Comfort's books. Please add $4 for shipping within the United States. (You may freely listen to "Hell's Best Kept Secret" online.)

We also have an eighteen-videotape series called "Excellence in Evangelism," which many churches are using to train their people. This comes with a free study guide.

To order products, or for a catalog of books, tracts, tapes, and videos by Ray Comfort, call (800) 437-1893, visit our website at www.raycomfort.com, or write to:

Living Waters Publications
P. O. Box 1172
Bellflower, CA 90706

Please note: This book is available at a low-cost bulk rate. Please consider giving copies of this publication to Christian friends and leaders within the Body of Christ.

Notes

1. While Charles Finney has his critics for his convictions regarding "revivals," and some even see him as the father of much of modern evangelism, we cannot ignore his insightful convictions when they are indisputably in line with the Word of God.

2. I see nothing unbiblical about a call to the altar for prayer. However, I believe that it is a great mistake to use music to stir a response. Music plays to the emotions of the human heart. It can produce fear, peace, joy, tension, etc., and can easily bring us to tears. Think of it like this: A little child has broken something I told him not to touch. I soberly challenge him with, "I told you not to touch that. *Are you sorry for what you have done?* Before you say anything, let me put on some gentle music to help you make up your mind." That would stir his emotions, when instead I should be appealing to his will and conscience.

3. Reidhead Publications, Box 556, Denton, MD 21629.

4. The audiotape version of "Hell's Best Kept Secret" can be heard free online at www.raycomfort.com.

5. For further teaching on how to use the Law to bring the knowledge of sin, see my books *Hell's Best Kept Secret* (Whitaker) and *How to Win Souls and Influence People* (Bridge-Logos).

6. The woman at the well is often cited to justify that we come to Jesus for happiness. However, to say that the "thirst" spoken of in John 4:13–15 is a thirst for happiness is mere conjecture. The *biblical* reason we come to the Savior is for *righteousness*, not happiness. Jesus said that those who hunger and thirst for *righteousness* are blessed (Matthew 5:6). He said that unless our *righteousness* exceeds that of the scribes and Pharisees, we wouldn't enter the kingdom of heaven. He told us to seek first the kingdom of God and His *righteousness*. This woman had transgressed the Seventh Commandment, and without

the *righteousness* of Christ, she would perish. The Law makes us thirst after a righteousness that we have no desire for.

7. This would seem to be another reference to the fact that false converts sit in the midst of the kingdom of God. In Revelation 18:2, "birds" are likened to the demonic realm.

8. Matthew Henry says of Luke 13:21: "This shall have its accomplishment in the destruction of the corrupt and hypocritical part of the Church" (*Matthew Henry's Bible Commentary*, p. 1191). In reference to Leviticus 23:17, where two loaves of bread in a "wave offering" contain leaven, *Ungers Bible Dictionary* says: "The two wave loaves typifying the Church contain leaven because there is evil in the Church" (Moody Press, p. 652).